Divine Timing
Dangers of
Premature Exposure

Bishop Nicholas Duncan-Williams

Divine Timing
Dangers of
Premature Exposure

Bishop Nicholas Duncan-Williams

Copyright © 2002

ISBN:1-56229-196-3

Pneuma Life Publishing
4423 Forbes Blvd
Lanham, MD 20706
www.PneumaLife.com

CONTACT INFORMATION FOR ARCHBISHIP DUNCAN-WILLIAMS

USA:
Action Worship Center
9759 Mountain Laurel Way
#18
Laurel, MD 20723
Phone: 410-379-5300
Fax: 301-498-7503

GHANA:
Christian Action Faith Ministries
P.O. Box 9527
K.I.A. ACCRA
Ghana, West Africa
Phone: 233-21-507-867
Fax: 233-21-507-860

LONDON:
Action Chapel
P.O. Box 346
Edgware, Middlesex, England
Ha8 6NW
Phone: 44-208-951-0626
Fax: 44-208-951-0662

Contents

Introduction

Dedication

I dedicate this book to Bishop T.D. Jakes. A man who is moving nations and impacting millions of lives around the world, because of his ability to discern divine timing.

Introduction

As a servant of God with over two decades of experience in Christian ministry, I have seen the Lord do awesome things in countless lives, and in many nations. I've seen Him raise men and women, like myself, who were nothing, and make giants and world shakers out of them. I am a living testimony and I confidently believe that indeed, "He raises the poor from the dust and lifts the needy from the dunghill. He seats them with princes and has them inherit a throne of honor" (I Sam.2:8). In the same way, I see God raising people from all walks of life to fulfill His end-time commission with an anointing and power the earth has never witnessed nor experienced.

However, I also see an enemy, who throughout the ages uses whatever means possible to defer, undermine, and if possible, stop the purposes of God. We should not be ignorant of his devices, lest he takes advantage of us and attacks us with one of his most subtle and underestimated weapons: lack of understanding of divine timing. The devil has successfully used this weapon against the people God uses for thousands of years and is still using it today.

We live in a computer age, where most things can be obtained in an instant. Although this "age" has its advantages, this 'quick-fix', 'drive-through', 'got-to-have-it-now', 'instant-this', 'instant-that' attitude has undermined adequate preparation, resulting in premature exposures. Many have fallen on this treacherous sword.

The breakdown of families, and soaring divorce rates can also be attributed to the fact that many people enter into marriage without knowing each other well enough but unwilling to wait for the process of time to unfold character traits of their spouse to be. Others force their children and fiancés into marriages when they have not taken time to prepare adequately, and divorce has been the result. This is true in the case of mothers who place undue pressure on their daughters to produce for them grandchildren before they die and younger women trapping men into marriage through pregnancy.

A lot of wealthy people die and bequeath wealth to children who are unable to properly manage them because they haven't been adequately trained to handle that responsibility. This wealth conferred on the children is intended to make them victors but has instead made them victims by luring them into wild lifestyles that eventually destroy them. This is also evident in other positions of trust in society.

Nations have suffered terrible consequences all over the world, especially those of the third world, and worst of all, Africa. This is because some leaders were prematurely exposed to power through the barrel of the gun. The result of such exposure has been the inability to handle power, thus destroying the ancient landmarks and leaving posterity with no secure future.

The Lord Jesus Christ left a priceless and powerful legacy for the Church. From generation to generation the apostles and men like Smith Wigglesworth, Lester Sumrall, Archbishop Benson Idahosa, and many others have also contributed to and left a rich legacy for the church. It will take people who have insight into divine timing and who are willing to move in step with the Holy Spirit to be able to carry on from where others left off. And should Jesus tarry, such will leave a more powerful legacy behind when it's time for them to also leave the scene.

The grave consequences of premature exposure cannot be overemphasized. Precious lives have been caught in its unyielding grip in their quest to "make it" overnight. Many more are skating on thin ice and drawing closer and closer to destruction at break-neck speed, ignoring all cautions of inadequate preparation and timing that are staring them in the face.

The Spirit of the Lord is upon me, for He has anointed me to blow the trumpet in Zion and sound an alarm on His holy hill pertaining to premature exposure. He has directed me to deliver people from the mistakes of their past, secure their 'now', and anchor their future and that of generations yet unborn. Through this book, one will find truths that will help to discern one's location on God's calendar and offer intelligent solutions based on God's Word.

Chapter 1

Origin of Time

Knowing the origin of something gives one a better understanding of it. On the other hand, ignorance of the purpose of anything will result in its inevitable abuse, and time is no exception. To fully understand time and its origins, we must go to the book of beginnings - where it all began. Time came out of eternity and will eventually give way to eternity. God is a Spirit and dwells in eternity. Before time, God was, and after time, He will still be. He is the same, yesterday, today, and forever.

The Scriptures make it apparent that time came into being by divine mandate when God decided to create man in His image and likeness. Time came into reality to fulfill a purpose. This was manifested when God came on the scene amidst the cosmic chaos and said,

"Let there be light and there was light... and God divided the light from the darkness and God called the light Day and the darkness He called Night and evening and morning was the first day" (Gen. 1:3-5)

All things were created, by Him and without Him was nothing made that was made (John 1:2). Therefore, in obedience to His commands, eternity gave birth to time by the undertaking of God's Spirit and His spoken Word.

Everything on planet Earth is here for a purpose (Eccl. 3:1). If it did not have a purpose, it would not have manifested in time. It's for this same reason that I submit to you that you are not simply a living entity, but are alive for a clear-cut and unique purpose. That is why you have manifested in time. Time was created for us and we were created to worship and fellowship with God.

God, in His infinite wisdom has set seasons, which come with their unique natures, outlooks, demands, and special levels of grace. This setting of seasons makes it easier to undertake the activities that help creation fulfill its purpose. Misunderstanding of times and seasons will result in their abuse. The abuse of time impairs the manifestation of purpose, and for this reason, the importance of understanding God's timing cannot be overstressed.

Importance of Time

Dr. Morris Cerullo, one of today's leading Christian ministers maintains, "The key to spiritual breakthrough is timing". One has to be in tune with the Holy Spirit, in order to secure major breakthroughs in life. Premature exposure, which is moving ahead of God's perfect timing, is the focus of this book.

Appreciating the importance of time and time management is one of the major indicators that distinguish successful people. Nature operates with a remarkable sense of timing, which reveals the mystery of God's word and power. The sun knows when to rise and set, ants know when to gather and, birds know when to migrate without any human interference or organization (Jer. 8:7).

Life has natural seasons summer, autumn, winter, and spring, or as in the tropics, dry (hot) and rainy (cold) seasons. Understanding these seasons enables one to prepare under different conditions and accomplish goals. Understanding this also helps because the demands of one season differ from those of another. A perfect illustration of this is clothing. You certainly would not wear boots and a wool coat in tropical weather. Knowing the rainy and dry seasons helps farmers know when to clear the land, sow, and harvest. Jesus said, "I must work... whilst it is day, the night cometh when no man can work."(John 9:4)

Understanding the importance of time is the springboard for true and lasting success; if there is true success then there can also be false success, the kind that lasts for a season.

Everyone was created for a purpose and was given an exact time to fulfill that purpose (Ps. 40:7). When this time is not used for its intended purpose, it is wasted and lost forever. What makes this issue crucial is that at the end of the age everyone will stand before God to give an account of what they did with their time on earth (Rom. 14:12).

Think about that for a moment, and ask yourself what you have done with your time so far. The importance of time, understood and used for the right purpose, determines the final destiny of souls.

Everyone is a steward of time, and time does not belong to anyone. For with man, time begins when he is born and ends when he dies. Having an understanding of time gives one fulfillment as well as success. Using time unproductively is almost suicidal. I challenge you to burn time and give light to your world!

Everyone on earth has 24 hours in a day, and 7 days in a week. What distinguishes one from another is the premium that one places on time.

You are where you are because of what you did yesterday with your time, and where you will be tomorrow is determined by what you are doing with your time today.

According to Dr Mike Murdock, one of the leading motivational preachers today, "insight about your future is hidden in your daily routine". Look at your daily routine critically and you will gain some understanding about your future. Knowledge of divine timing will make you outstand, and give you great advantage over others. It will usher you into leadership and equip you with wisdom. "They that have understanding shall lead many".

Chapter 2

Knowing Divine Timing

As a preacher, a question that I am often asked is "How does one understand divine timing or know God's timing?" Before we look at how one can perceive divine timing, let's establish a basis, which will enhance our understanding.

God's understanding of time is different from ours. "For a day to the Lord is like a thousand years and a thousand years as one day unto the Lord", (2 Pet 3:8). Also the Scriptures say, "for a thousand years in thy sight are but yesterday when it is past and a watch in the night," (Psalm 90). In God's sight beauty is equal to maturation and perfection, "...for He makes all things beautiful in His time" (Eccl. 3:11) - not our time, but His time. This is where many people miss God. We have personal conceptions and perceptions of time, which differ from God's. We must have the mind of Christ in order to understand His divine timing.

Discovery of Purpose

There are several ways of understanding divine timing. The discovery of one's reason for existence helps in this regard. The reason why so many people commit suicide is that they don't see a reason to live they don't have the perception of God nor His purpose for their lives. As a result of this ignorance they subscribe to the devil's suggestion to end it all. When you understand your purpose, you can stand up and boldly declare in the face of any situation or circumstance that, "I shall not die, but live to declare the works of the Lord in the land of the living (Ps 118:17).

When one discovers purpose, one will begin to understand time. People who know their purpose have insight about what should be done and usually work to fulfill it. They do not concern themselves about many things; instead, they focus, plan, and make the best use of time. I encourage you to discover your reason for being.

As a young boy, I attempted many crazy things in a bid to "make it" and to be fulfilled in life. I almost died and in the process, I lost three fingers on my right hand, an experience which brought me into contact with a nurse who led me to the Lord. From the moment I received Christ and got hold of the purpose for my being, time became meaningful to me.

When you apprehend your purpose, you can't quit or complain about being tired, but must keep pressing on and ignore all opposition until you have completed your assignment.

Observation

Understanding divine timing also comes through careful observation. One's ability to observe indicators and interpret time, or events that carry a message, can help in understanding divine timing. All truth is parallel. When one observes the sunrise or sunset, one can understand what time it is and take the necessary steps to do what is required for that time.

"And he said also to the people, "When ye see a cloud rise out of the west, straightway ye say, There cometh a shower and so it is. And when ye see the south wind blow, ye say, There will be heat; and it cometh to pass. Ye hypocrites, ye can discern the face of the sky and of the earth, but how is it that ye do not discern this time? (Luke 12:54-56)

Divine Encounter

A divine encounter as experienced in dreams, visions, trances, angelic visitations or the manifestation of the personality of Jesus helps one to understand divine timing. Many Bible characters had such experiences, and many still do today. Men like Jacob, who was later called Israel, understood the time to leave Laban's house through a divine encounter (Gen.31:11-13).

Jesus, in the Jordan after the baptism, had an encounter with the Holy Spirit and knew it was time to wait on the Father in the wilderness before launching out into ministry. Through a divine encounter at Mount Horeb, Moses, after 40 years of wandering in the wilderness, came to understand God's divine timing for the deliverance of the people of Israel. He grasped the purpose of his being and became a deliverer.

The angel of the Lord also helped Joseph, the husband of Mary, know when and what steps to take to save the life of Jesus. These visitations or divine encounters gave the people knowledge and understanding of God's timing for their lives, families, and assignments on earth.

My prayer is that through the pages of this book you will have revelation that will prepare you for a divine encounter for your own life and all that concerns you.

The Word Of God

The Word of God or Scriptures can make one discern God's timing. Scripture reveals, "I Daniel understood by the books" through the prophecies of Jeremiah the time for the turning of the captivity of God's people in Babylon (Dan. 9:2).

Through God's Word one can gain understanding into God's timing for one's life, family and nation. David said, Through thy precepts I get understanding: therefore I hate every false way, (Psalms 119:104). The Word of God is the manual for living and it has exact and very accurate information on the times in which we live and the future.

The Scriptures point out significant events in the history of mankind. An example is the coming together of the European Union, which will set the stage to bring the One World Government in the future as predicted by Daniel. (Dan 8:9-14)

The spiritual time for the church today is also clearly painted by the Scripture:

In the last days perilous times shall come, for men shall be lovers of themselves, lovers of money, boasters, proud, blasphemers, disobedient to parents, unthankful, unholy, unloving, unforgiving, slanderous, without self control, brutal, despisers of good things, traitors, head-

strong, haughty, lovers of pleasures rather than lovers of God, having a form of godliness but denying the power thereof (2 Tim 3:1-5).

Thank God that the Scriptures declare that Jesus is coming back for a glorious church and that the church shall be "raptured" in power and not in weakness and defeat (Eph. 5:2-7). The reason the devil wants to keep you from the Word of God is the information in it that can equip you with insight about God's timing for your life and all He has made available for you to enjoy.

Bible Prophecy

If you want to know about future events and know the times you must turn to the thousands of prophecies in the Bible. History has proven the extraordinary and unerring accuracy of Bible prophecy. In the book of Daniel, chapter 12, the Bible speaks of the Great Tribulation in verse 1, the Resurrection in verse 2, and the rewards of the righteous in verse 3.

Then, in verse 4, the Bible reads, "But thou O Daniel, shut up the words and seal the book even to the time of the end. Many shall run to and fro, and knowledge shall be increased." The subject of the Great Tribulation, the Resurrection, and the Rewards of the righteous are all events that will surely take place in the end-time. Also in verse 13, the Bible reads, "But go thou way till the end be, for thou shall rest and stand in thy lot at the end of the day." This was to tell Daniel, that the prophecy was not for his time, and that he would pass away before its fulfillment.

Looking at the prophecy, "...Many shall run to and fro, and knowledge shall be increased..." we can see the clear fulfillment of these events in our days. The rate at which many people are running to and fro, by traveling from place to place for trade and for tourism is unprecedented. This is because of the awesome transition in our means of transportation. We've gone from camels to locomotive trains and from wagons to planes. Now we have more modernized trains, cars, and airplanes that travel at amazing speeds- some even faster than the speed of sound. This has made traveling easier, faster and more convenient. We even have the technology that can take man to the moon in a relatively short time.

The second part of the prophecy, which talks about knowledge being increased, is also fulfilled in our day. Never in any age has knowledge increased and continued at an amazing extent as it has in our age. Statistics show that almost five million books are published every year, and that the total store of human knowledge doubles every eight years.

The amazing increase in knowledge can be attributed to the sophisticated and high-powered computers, complex instruments and equipment that have been invented for conducting research, accessing information, and disseminating information. Whatever the means of increased knowledge, it was predicted about 534 BC, by the prophet Daniel in the Bible.

Jesus was asked by His disciples, as He sat on the Mount of Olives in Matthew 24:3, when the temple would be destroyed, and the signs for his coming, made certain predictions. In verse 6 of Matthew 24, the Bible says, "And when ye shall hear of wars and rumors of wars see that ye be not troubled for all these must come to pass, but the end is not yet."

History reveals that there have been several wars over the centuries, but the greatest escalation took place in the 20th century. Until 1914, war had never universalized. After World War I and World War II, we saw this fulfilled, and everyone thought it was over.

On the contrary, there have been major wars that have claimed over 23 million lives. In 1993 alone, 29 major wars were fought. "Nations rising against nation" could be interpreted as ethnic group against ethnic group. This is evident in wars between ethnic groups all over Africa, Yugoslavia, and the Gulf region to name a few. Jesus predicted these in verse 7. "For nation shall rise against nation and kingdom against kingdom, and there shall be famine, pestilence, and earthquakes in diverse places." Throughout the 1990s, 100 million people died through starvation. The World Health Organization statistics indicate that one third of the world is well fed, one third is underfed, and one third is starving. Presently, over 4 million die annually through starvation. This is a clear indication of the famine Jesus talked about centuries ago. Pestilence in the form of AIDS that has plagued over 40 million people, along with other deadly diseases, has emerged in our day.

Biblical prophecy can give one an excellent picture of God's timings for the future.

Personal Prophecy

A prophecy or a prophetic word from a servant of God can make one understand divine timing. Through the prophet Isaiah, King Hezekiah was told to put his house in order because he was going to die, and through the same prophet he was told that his life had been extended for 15 more years (2 Kings 20:1). If Hezekiah knew his time through a prophetic word, so can you.

Nathan, the prophet of God, encouraged King David in his plans to build a temple for God when David asked him for counsel. This was a good and godly idea, and many of us today would have encouraged such a venture. But on God's calendar, the timing was premature. King David's assignment, in line with God's will, did not include building God's temple, although he would have loved to do so. God, later, intervened and spoke to Nathan, the prophet, that He had not ordained David to build the temple, but rather Solomon, his son.

This prophetic word enabled David to understand divine timing and also God's will concerning the temple. It saved him from frustration, unnecessary resistance and the needless pressure he would have faced if he had gone ahead with the project. He needed the prophetic word and an understanding of the time. He would have been trying to do something to please God, without God's approval.

If national leaders sought God concerning His expectation of them, while in office, they would accomplish much and bring great prosperity, peace and blessing upon their people.

"The Lord will do nothing without first revealing it to His servants, the prophets." (Amos 3:7)

Although God has used me to give direction concerning God's timing to nations, churches and individuals, I will caution, that in spite of the above mode of knowing divine timing, God expects every born-again Christian in the New Testament Church, to hear his voice. Jesus said, "My sheep hear my voice..." I always encourage people to seek God for confirmation regarding what they are told. I do not encourage people to pursue prophets and coerce them for a word.

Every prophecy, apart from biblical predictions, is subject to change. Every prophecy should be judged in the light of Scripture, and should not be like fortune-telling, mind-reading, palm-reading, etc., where the so-called "prophets" prophesy at will. That is demonic and is not of God. Prophecy should be inspired by the Holy Spirit, judged, and be in accordance with God's Word.

There are many false prophets on the loose and it would serve us well to be cautious in receiving and obtaining personal prophecies bearing in mind that anything contrary to the word, is steering us away from God.

Prayer & Fasting

Seeking the Lord by waiting on Him through fasting and prayer is a wonderful and powerful tool in understanding God's timing for one's life. David sought God often through fasting and prayer and never lost a battle because he understood divine timing and knew when and how to make a move. He always inquired of the Lord (2 Sam. 5:17-25).

Through prayer and fasting you can also understand divine timing for your life and live a victorious Christian life because you know God's timing and can also anticipate the enemy's move to avoid defeat. "For they that seek the Lord understand all things" (Prov. 18:5). All things include understanding times and seasons. God says, "Call to me (prayer) and I will answer you and tell you great and unsearchable things that you do not know"

(Jer 33:3). There are secrets about your life, future, and the times that God is waiting to reveal to you, if you will only call upon Him.

The Bible recalls that John, the Revelator, was in the Spirit on the Lord's Day on the isle of Patmos, "...and he heard a voice behind him saying..." (Rev. 1:10-11). Anytime you are determined to seek God's face and pray, with fasting, you will hear His voice, which will give you direction and insight into the times and seasons.

David said, "...my times are in his hand...." He also said, " I have come to do thine will O God as it is written of me in the volumes of the books" (Psalm 40:7). Through these Scriptures, we understand that everybody's time is in the Lord's hand, and He knows the end from the beginning. If you come before him, He will reveal to you portions of His blueprint for your life. There is a book written concerning you in eternity before you came into time. That's why He knew your end before you were born.

I strongly admonish you to understand divine timing concerning what He has for you by discovering God's purpose and His assignment for you. Following this, carefully observe indicators that interpret time. Ensure that all your actions, are governed by the Word of God, and be sensitive to the times that we are in, as indicated through biblical prophecy. Establish fellowship in a Bible-believing church, where the Holy Spirit is moving, and seek God earnestly through prayer and fasting. This will strategically position you for a mind-blowing and destiny-changing encounter with God that will cause you to know the times and seasons of your life and place you in your destiny.

It would be a great mistake and sin to remain ignorant of what God expects of you after receiving this truth. Rise up now and don't let go of God, until you are fully in the flow of His plans.

Chapter 3

Premature Exposure to Political Power

Dominion and power, glory and honor belong to the most-high God. He is the Lord of Lords, and the epitome of all rule and authority. His Most Excellency, I AM, The King of kings reigns forever and ever.

God created man in His own image and after His likeness; this means that He wanted man to not only possess His image but also exhibit His nature.

Now, if God is King then He expects his children to be kings and reign in every facet of this life. That is why those redeemed by the Lord have been made kings and priests, and are referred to as a royal priesthood. If it is too hard for one to grasp what God has in mind pertaining to His children, just look at Adam's dominion before his fall and the reign of Jesus while He was on earth.

God is interested in all nations, "for the kingdom is the Lord's: and He is the governor among the nations" (Ps

22:28). God charts the course of nations. God has a political calendar at every level of authority and rule, and as the King of the nations, has the blueprint for the politics of every nation, tribe, tongue, kindred, and people.

To be able to move in line with God's political will, one must know the mind of God. God controls the rise and fall of leaders. He sets up kings and removes kings. Remember, it's not men, or cabinets, or elections, but it is God who sets up and removes kings. He uses men, circumstances, and other available channels to establish His purpose. Jesus said to Pilate, "...you have no power over me (as king) except it is given to you from above" (John 19:11). That means Pilate's authority, as king, was from heaven not earth.

Many people including some believers seek to separate God from politics. They believe that God has nothing to do with politics and politics has nothing to do with God. This mentality is a subtle deception, because God is King and He is the source of all power including political power.

God reveals to his servants certain events concerning nations. About 200 years, long before Cyrus was born, God had already "set him up" as king, and spoken through His prophet Isaiah and given details pertaining to his reign and assignment.

> *"Thus saith the Lord to his anointed to Cyrus, whose right hand I have holden, to subdue nations before him; and I will loose the loins of kings, to open before him the two leaved gates; and the gates shall not be shut; I will go before thee, and make the crooked places straight; I will break in pieces the gates of brass, and cut in sunder the bars of iron: And I will give thee the treasures of darkness, and hidden riches of secret places, that thou mayest know that I, the Lord, which call thee by name, am the God of Israel. For Jacob my servant's sake, and Israel*

mine elect, I have even called thee by name: I have surnamed thee,
though thou hast not known me". (Isaiah 45:1-4)

This same truth is illustrated in the life of the prophet
Jeremiah. God told Jeremiah, "Before I formed thee in the
belly I knew thee and before thou camest forth out of the
womb I sanctified thee and I ordained thee a prophet unto
the nations" (Jer.1:5). In the same way, Cyrus, was
ordained king before he was born. That is why God could
speak it 200 years before he was born, and it came to pass.
The same was true of King Josiah of Israel, who reigned in
640 BC. Over 280 years before he was born, during the
reign of King Jeroboam around 922 BC, his birth, rule, and
assignment were prophesied. The Scriptures also reveal
that God made Nebuchadnezzar king of Babylon and
Daniel testified of this in his presence saying,

Thou O king art a king of kings for the God of heaven hath given thee
a kingdom, power, and strength and glory...and hath made thee ruler
over them all (Daniel 2:37,38).

Not only did Daniel testify to this, but after being humbled by God for seven years, Nebuchadnezzar himself
realized that man had not given him Kingship but God
himself had. Let's take a moment and examine the testimony of Nebuchadnezzar, one of history's most powerful
political leaders.

"And at the end of my days I Nebuchad-nezzar lifted up mine eyes
unto heaven, and mine understanding returned unto me, and I blessed
the Most High, and I praised and honored him that liveth forever,
whose dominion is an everlasting dominion, and his kingdom is from
generation to generation. And all the inhabitants of the earth are reput-
ed as nothing, and he doeth according to his will in the army of heav-
en, and among the inhabitants of the earth and none can stay his hand,
or say unto him, What doest thou? At the same time my reason
returned unto me and for the glory of my kingdom in mine honor and

brightness returned unto me; and I was established in my kingdom, and excellent majesty was added unto me. Now I Nebuchadnezzar praise and extol and honor the King of heaven, all whose works are truth and his ways judgment: and those that walk in pride he is able to abase."
(Daniel 4:34-37)

He acknowledged that God had done all these things for him. That is why he praised God for establishing him in his kingdom as the king. God has not changed. He is the same yesterday, today and forever. God used Nebuchadnezzar to set an example for future kings and political leaders. The angel gives the reason for this, which is,

"To the intent that the living may know that the Most High ruleth in the kingdom of men and giveth it to whomsoever He will and setteth up over it the basest of men" (Dan. 4:17)

Therefore we can confidently say that God has a plan and, has set times for those plans as far as politics is concerned. This applies to all levels of political office from international to local levels.

Daniel saw the various kingdoms and their strengths revealed in his visions. God foreordained David, king of Israel, Hazel, king of Aram (who prematurely took office (II Kings 8:7-14), Nebuchadnezzar, king of Babylon, and Joseph, Prime Minister in Egypt. And He is still in control and in the process of placing and removing people from office.

If you are foreordained to serve in a political arena, may the Lord show you, as you read this book, what your destiny is.

Many have misconceptions of the type of authority that existed then as compared to that which is exercised today. Kings, in biblical times, exercised what would be referred to, today, as executive, legislative and judicial powers. They were also the commanders-in-chief of their armies. Some controlled vast territories from Ethiopia to India and their mode of operation couldn't be said to be any different from what is happening today. It even appears that they had more wealth, power and sovereignty than our current political leaders.

God was so concerned about the political office that He outlined specifications and also precautions to be taken into consideration when a king was being placed in office (Deut. 17:14-20). A careful study of this should guide Christians everywhere in their choice of a king or political authority. When we follow the above commands of God as a guiding principle in our choice of leaders, it allows God to have His way in politics for our benefit. We ought to follow the admonition of the Holy Spirit through Paul to "...pray first for kings and all in authority...(I Tim. 2:1,2)".

Sons and daughters with great potential, talents, leadership abilities, contacts, and influence, have been destroyed by premature political exposure. Some have ended up hurting themselves or the very people they intended to serve. These have been precious people with great political aspirations and pregnant with dreams and visions. Many of such pains could have been avoided if they had waited for God's perfect timing or lay hold of the type of information you are reading right now, and heeded its advice.

Premature exposure frequently occurs in the realm of politics and has to be addressed since it affects many lives and the destinies of nations. Humanity has suffered unimaginable pain throughout history because of prematurity in politics. The continent of Africa has witnessed, and is still witnessing some of the worst forms of anarchy, dictatorship, and tyranny because people were prematurely exposed to power. The result has been abuse or intoxication under the influence of power even to the point of insanity.

In their insatiable lust for power some will do anything and will not desist from using the most savage, crude, barbaric, unethical, and inhumane ways of achieving their ends. It could be through the barrel of a gun, satanic manipulations, and other forms of diabolic armament. The result has been indescribable sufferings and seemingly incurable wounds inflicted on countless lives. No wonder many nations are now considering national healing and reconciliation, which can only come through forgiveness and the power of Jesus and His blood.

Premature exposure to political power has been a major root of the African leadership crisis and the archenemy of peace and stability of democracy. A careful study of the political history of Africa, especially in my nation Ghana, will reveal this. Thankfully, this is being corrected through prayer, fasting, and skillful intercession by the saints. Our history is strewn with many examples people coming into power overnight and without knowing how to handle the pressures and weighty issues that came with the position. These unwarranted promotions always created imbalance, strife, agitation, and chaos. It also undermined justice, which resulted in all forms of political unrest.

Rebels, revolutionaries, and soldiers in various parts of Africa have seized power, or tried to seize power through military coups. They have tried to do this without understanding the dynamics of government, international politics, and public administration. They were not willing to go through the school of discipline and patience so they would be able to handle the challenges and pressures of leadership. Their ignorance, immaturity, and inexperience resulted in untold hardships for their entire subregion or citizenry. Examples abound, and we continue to see or hear them through the media everyday.

Although the political process in developed countries is not void of faults, it helps its people and promotes maturity in leadership. This enhances growth, stability, peace, productivity, prosperity and accountability. The process to the throne or any helm of political authority is well defined and carefully structured to allow people to work their way up and grow through the ranks while learning, maturing, and gaining experience along the way.

In the U.S., for example, there are the House of Representatives as well as the Senate, which are made up of men and women with great experience and knowledge to help govern the nation. There is also accountability for every power, a practice that reduces the abuse of power. In this case, an amateur does not become a leader. Now, if those who have worked their way to the top with such a rich store of knowledge still make mistakes, then the nation whose leaders haven't been through the process stands at greater risk.

God never intended for amateurs to rule His people or be in leadership. In exceptional cases, God has made provision for the prematurely exposed leader, by providing him with guidance until they are matured enough to handle things themselves.

> **Oh, how I pray that you and I, together with God, will help establish such systems in our communities through prayer and action.**

"Now I say that the heir, as long as he is a child differeth nothing from a servant though he be lord of all but is under tutors and governors until the time appointed of the Father" (Gal. 4:1,2). Whenever people find themselves in such a position, they need to seek God, find His will and allow Him to guide them to godly and mature people, who can help them make the right decisions and they shall not fail "...for in the multitude of godly counselors there is safety" (Prov. 24:6).

Anyone who has not been prepared, tried, or groomed for a certain position should be considered dangerous when they expose themselves prematurely. Such people can harm themselves and others without realizing what they are doing.

As judgment and punishment to Israel, God said, "I will make boys their officials and mere children will govern them (Isa. 3:4,5). Here, it's clearly revealed that it is not God's will for children or amateurs to be in political office, but those who are mature. If we examine each of these situations we will find that each resulted in oppression, chaos, suffering, wickedness, anarchy, and brought a curse on the nation.

For it is written, "Woe to you, O land, whose king is a child and whose princes feast in the morning..." (Eccl. 10:16) That child refers to rulers or leaders who are immature or childish. Children, by nature, are selfish, and are not able to exert control over their emotions and appetites. One basic characteristic of childish or immature leadership is its desire to satisfy its own appetites and cravings before taking care of the needs of the people.

According to the Scriptures, a nation with such political leaders is cursed and doomed. To the nations whose leaders are mature, God says, "And blessed are you O land whose king is of noble birth and whose princes eat at the proper time for strength and not for drunkenness". (Eccl. 10:17) Here, the king of noble birth is one who, by virtue of his background, has been trained, well groomed, prepared and nurtured from infancy as heir to the position.

Let's look at some accounts that show the outcome of premature political exposure and inadequate preparation on nations. "And the Lord said to Samuel, "How long will thou mourn for Saul seeing I have rejected him from reigning over Israel. Fill thine horn with oil and go...for I have me a king amongst his sons" (1Sam. 16:1). Saul, the first king of Israel, was a "ready-made" king. From nowhere, with very little or no preparation, he was anointed king of Israel. He never had the opportunity to grow into it. Saul's kingship was not planned because it was not the appointed time for Israel to have a king. The people introduced the institution of kingship prematurely and God wasn't in favor of it, for reasons stated in the Book of I Samuel.

The major reason could be that according to God's original plan, kingship was to proceed from Judah, ". . . the scepter shall not depart from Judah until Shiloh comes" (Gen. 49:10). This indicates that Judah was supposed to provide kings for Israel. Some schools of thought believe that had it not been for the mistake of Judah, the book of Judges would not have been included in Israel's political history.

Scripture tells us that Judah slept with Tamar (his daughter-in-law) and gave birth to Perez and Zerah. According to Jewish law, an offspring from such a relationship was a bastard, and a bastard was not allowed to enter into the congregation of the Lord, even to the tenth generation. (Deut.23: 2) Thus until the tenth generation, none of Judah's descendants could enter into the congregation of the Lord, as a result they could not function as kings. It is interesting to note that genealogically, David was the tenth descendant. (Matt.1:3-6)

I believe the devil was insistent on interfering with God's plans so as to undermine God's purpose and perfect will. He incited the nation of Israel by employing their emotions and their carnal desires to press Samuel for a king prematurely. Out of love and concern for Israel, God tried to dissuade them by giving them details of what their king would do. He did this so they would change their minds but they still didn't want God's choice and perfect will. You may ask yourself, "Didn't God choose Saul as king?" The answer is that Israel compelled God to give them a king. God gave the people what they wanted and not what He wanted.

There are times when God allows certain things, not because it is His perfect will, but because of the stubbornness of men. Thus, men sometimes press out of God's perfect will and His goodwill and find themselves in His acceptable or permissive will. Apparently, the institution of the monarchy, with Saul being the head, was premature as Saul was of the tribe of Benjamin. The Scriptures show that God's perfect will was to produce a king from the tribe of Judah.

It is worth noting that it is possible to introduce an entire political process prematurely, creating disorder for a period of time.

Let's examine a practical situation in current times to illustrate that this gross error is not isolated to just biblical Israel. In Africa, it is easy for a political or economic process to be superimposed by the powers that be. There is the need to patiently introduce a political process that addresses the complexity of the political situation.

The root of the Rwanda-Burundi crisis could be attributed to the premature exposure of their political system. This has created numerous problems for the people of Rwanda, resulting in the loss of over 3 million lives. And still the situation has not been completely addressed.

Let's get to the root so we can see how to deal with this issue. History recalls that the indigenous people were the Batwas who constitute 1% of the entire population. The Hutus (approx. 90% of population) were farmers who also settled there. The Tutsis were warriors who came and settled there later.   The Tutsis were very rich, politically powerful, militarily wise, and educated.   The Hutus worked for them as farmers and served them without trouble as both benefited. When the Dutch came and introduced education, challenges emerged but the situation became distressed when Rwanda gained her independence, and democracy was introduced.

Though it was good, I believe it was premature because with democracy, the majority carries the vote. The Tutsis were the minority. They had more power, wealth, and military strength because of predominance in the army. They felt superior and were not willing to submit to the

Hutus, who had gained political power through the election. The military felt threatened, and opposed the system that was set in motion along with its democratic tenets. There were Tutsis in neighboring countries; who helped their brothers oppose the system, which further complicated the issue, from a national to a regional, ethnic conflict. The battle still rages on, becoming more complex and more atrocious as the days go by.

Unfortunately, Rwanda did not have the structures and political make-up to maturely address the sensitive needs of the people.   Rwanda, like Israel, introduced its democratic government prematurely. Saul was a "man-made" king when he was put on the throne. This, coupled with his own weakness, caused him to be rejected by God, and his end was tragic. Premature exposure and short cuts to power without the process can ultimately lead to tragedies.

To rectify Israel's situation, God rejected Saul and anointed David. David was anointed when he was only 15 years old. God allowed King Saul to occupy the throne for a while after his rejection, and used him to prepare David for the throne. So from the time God said, "He had provided Himself a king amongst the sons of Jesse..." to the training of David for kingship, nearly 15 years had gone by.

Let's take a close look at God's school for maturing David and Joseph. David went through a rather long but necessary process to prepare him for kingship. David first served his father and brothers, cared for sheep, then played the harp for Saul, he later killed the lion and the bear and the progression is that he killed the giant Goliath. After that he became a captain in Saul's army, fought with the Philistines, and went on several military operations. He lived as a fugitive in Ziklag, then migrated to the cave of Adullam and then became king and ruled the tribe of Judah for 7 years in Hebron and eventually became king over Israel in Jerusalem.

What a trip and what process! Fifteen years of preparation made him ready to be the king God wanted him to be. He was the best king of Israel and his son Solomon succeeded him. Even with all that preparation David still made his mistakes while on the throne.

Joseph was 15 years old when he had a dream that his siblings would bow to him, but God had to prepare him first. This was how God prepared him; Joseph served his father and his brothers. He was sold into slavery to the Ishmaelites who then sold him to Potiphar, in whose house he became a caretaker and manager.

He was sent to prison on a lustful woman's fairytale and while he was there he served his fellow prisoners. Afterwards God raised him from prison to the palace where he was made governor of Egypt and the Prime Minister of the world's most powerful nation in his time.

Fifteen tedious years passed before Joseph saw the fulfillment of his dream. He did not occupy the position of Prime Minister of Egypt until he completed God's process of maturation. For Joseph the age of maturation was 30.

If you have a vision for political office and God has destined you for that office, don't be in haste because the place where you are may be your training ground. The training process was not limited to Joseph and David; it happened in the life of Kwame Nkrumah, Nelson Mandela, and many others. God has his ways.

David could have yielded to the temptation of premature exposure, politically. Not only because he knew he was God's choice, but also because he had the support of the people. It would have been easy for David to murder Saul in his palace and stage a mutiny. However, David, understanding divine timing, spared him. David never shed a drop of innocent blood to annex the throne. The Lord fought for him, took him there, and established him. God anointed him and appointed him in his season.

The spirits that fought your fathers and the administration before you will definitely fight you. You will find yourself facing the same problems challenges, battles and giants they faced and could not conquer. Waiting for the right time, and learning through preparation will give you the upper hand and place you in a position to overcome them. My admonition to all, especially, those who desire to take up positions of authority, is to take guidance from David's life. Learn the ways of God, become a man after God's own heart, and develop into one of the greatest leaders the world has ever known.

For those who are usually tempted to move before their time to seize power by force, let the case of Adonijah and Absalom be an indication of the possible consequences. Absalom was one of David's loved and trusted sons. He was an heir to the throne, wise and handsome. He later conspired with political activists, leaders in the existing government and even the most trusted confidants of the King, like Ahitophel.

With all Israel and some of the power brokers of the time behind him, he moved in to actually usurp the throne. He slept with his father's concubines openly and disgraced his father. He cunningly stole the hearts of the people by painting a negative picture of the existing authority. He later conspired with some powerful men and drove the king into the wilderness. He then mustered more troops to totally destroy him and the troops that were with him. His end was "self execution" because he had prematurely exposed himself.

The book of Kings reveals that execution is the end of most people who prematurely expose themselves. However, there are times when some succeed, but it comes at a great price, which sometimes hurts them throughout their entire lives. Such leaders will admit that this road is not easy, and the lives of those who do not admit it show that it's not worth it after all.

Premature exposure in politics, places the individual or sometimes a whole nation on a volcanic mountain whose explosive power and fury is relentless and provocative ready to unleash fire and destruction without warning. Apart from this danger, it also has the potential to affect already laid foundations and rob today's leaders of the ability to give the future generation a firm foundation.

It undermines strategic planning and proper programs that have a positive effect on the political future. It also creates a breeding ground for narrow-minded decisions that may prove successful for that moment but later become an obstacle to long lasting success. Decisions made by many who have prematurely exposed themselves in the arena of politics have destroyed great opportunities, wonderful privileges, strategic relationships and personalities.

A prematurely exposed leadership overlooks cautions, which are crucial to long lasting and ever increasing success. Let us not sabotage our political future and that of others by setting novices in positions of trust when more matured and qualified people could be solicited to help.

Our lives today will be lessons for posterity tomorrow. Doing the right thing may not always be easy, but we should also never forget that our lives today will be the written epistles in the future. Generations to come will look critically without fear or favor and pass judgment; making them either to bless or curse us, depending on whether we walk in truth and make sacrifices or in falsehood to gratify our passions and lust.

As you read this book you may have a political aspiration or know someone who does. My sincere prayer is that you will pray for God's perfect timing for exposure and God's grace to go through the process. Also remember to lift up those who are in leadership or intend to be in leadership within your community or nation that the perfect will of God is done in their lives.

Chapter 4

Premature Exposure to Money & Wealth

Premature exposure, in the area of finances, has been strongly impressed on my heart to address because of the power that money has and the way the enemy has employed it as a major weapon. The Bible says that, "...money answereth all things...." (Eccl. 10:19)

Money is powerful and has the ability to make or break you. It has been said that, "...money is a good servant, but a terrible master..." It is for this reason that premature exposure to wealth can destroy any person, great or small, old or young if they have not been adequately prepared to handle money.

One is prematurely exposed to wealth or economic power when one comes to possess these through legitimate or foul means at the wrong time. At a time when one does not possess the maturity, experience, emotional stability, financial expertise, or simple wisdom, one will ultimately be controlled by the wealth. This eventually leads to waste, loss and destruction.

A blessing becomes a snare when it brings compromise, enmity with God, ungodly associations, and damage to family relationships. Such conditions reflect premature exposure to wealth. An example is when someone is presented with a lucrative job opportunity or financial prospect that will be at the expense of ones spiritual life. The prospect is prematurely exposed if the blessing has the potential to damage the benefactor.

Today, it is not difficult to be prematurely exposed to wealth. Many dubious deals, fraudulent business transactions, as well as a host of get-rich-quick strategies abound thus creating a lot of problems, destroying a lot of families, and also affecting our nation. What is happening all over the world is alarming. People will do anything to get money. Many also defy all caution in a bid to enjoy or possess, within a moment what someone has labored for years to acquire. Our overcrowded State prisons are evident to this fact.

Statistics indicate that "economically-motivated" crimes account for over 60% of the prison's population and the underlying factor is the desire to get rich quickly. The quest to make money instantly or prematurely motivates people to employ all forms of degrading, unlawful and unethical means. This is destroying our society and sending able-bodied people behind bars and releasing them in a worse state than when they entered.

Premature exposure to wealth is a powerful predator that affects entire nations, businesses, well meaning adults and even children.

Gambling or lottery of any form offers premature or instant success. This is an easy way out of dissatisfaction, and now has been embraced and accepted to the extent that airports, restaurants and even restrooms give you the opportunity to "strike it rich". Sales executives have discovered raffles to be the most effective strategy to get people to patronize their products. Television bombards us with raffles, sweepstakes, and draws to inject false hope to those willing to listen. Gambling, in our society, is presented in diverse forms and packages and many addicted souls fall prey and can't break out of it because they desire so strongly to be millionaires overnight.

Apart from the numerous negative effects on families, those whose fathers and husbands are addicted to gambling will tell you how terrible it is. Statistics reveal that very few people have been able to make and maintain wealth gained from gambling apart from those who actually operate it.

Paradoxically, we see very caring and loving parents who ignorantly shower too much money on their children by introducing them to huge amounts of money at a tender age. This, in turn, makes spendthrifts out of the children. The children grow up accustomed to huge spending and they do not appreciate the toil that goes into creating wealth. Instead of being shrewd, they become prodigal. It is no wonder that many rich children are labeled, "spoiled brats" and are not able to live to the expectations of their parents.

Many people in courtship try to buy love by prematurely exposing their partners to money. When crisis comes, these partners leave because they have been prematurely exposed to money, which became the strength of their relationships. Men and women beware.

I believe in applying the keys of the kingdom to secure financial breakthroughs. I also believe that poverty does not glorify God, neither does it resemble piety. I know some people who live right and have done everything (giving, fasting, praying for finances) and still feel like they haven't been heard.

If you find yourself in such a position, be encouraged, for you have been heard on high. The answer to your prayer is set for an appointed time since its immediate manifestation could destroy you. God does not just give and bless in any fashion, but gives according to the person's ability to responsibly manage what has been given to them.

In the parable of the talents, we realize that God gave them money (not gifts as is usually interpreted). And the Scripture says, "he gave them according to their several abilities..." (Mat. 25:15). When this Scripture speaks of abilities, it means that not every one can handle certain amounts of money at a particular time successfully. If I would give my 8-year-old child, fifty thousand Dollars and my Mercedes Benz, he would waste my money and abuse my car and ultimately destroy himself. It is not because he is evil but because he is not mature enough to handle such responsibility.

God, by His nature, usually prepares people before he is gives them gifts. He told the disciples not to cast their "pearls before swine" (Matt. 7:6). It is, therefore not surprising that everyone who is a candidate for mega-prosperity goes through God's "school of preparation." In this fashion, they can really appreciate God as their source. What is equally important is, knowing how to manage what has been entrusted into their care. God is able to create something out of nothing. He loves to begin with you from zero and bring you to supernatural abundance, so that all will acknowledge that it is indisputably the doing of the Lord, and no one can take His glory.

When one has never been hungry, he does not really know how one feels when they complain to him of hunger. For when you have been hungry and poor and have been through certain situations, you are in a better position to empathize with those who are in the same situations.

Blessed be God ... who comforts us in all our tribulation, that we may be able to comfort them which are any trouble by the comfort wherewith we ourselves are comforted of God. (2 Cor 1:3-4)

Therefore, God deems it an absolute necessity to take those he intends to use in the area of finance, through preparation. After all, financial blessings are not yours to enjoy with your family alone but to help finance the purposes of God. Countless testimonies attest to the fact that many who have become wealthy and powerful, today, came from very humble beginnings, and went through very hard times, until God lifted and prospered them.

As a Bishop, I have seen many who were very humble, on fire for God, serviceable, punctual, and loved the Lord, their spouse and family until they, "got that job" or "broke through financially." All of a sudden, they started to serve mammon or their job and changed drastically. Their commitment toward God and their families waxed cold as they became more in love with the blessing, than with the one who gave the blessing. Generally, these people may have deserved the blessing that came to them, but their inability to handle it reveals that it came prematurely.

Apart from God's genuine blessing being handled the wrong way, the devil, also knows how to employ and use premature exposure to destroy many. If the devil knows that giving you a job, money, or some sort of financial breakthrough, before your time will get you off his back, he will make every effort to sway you into accepting his offer.

Have you noticed that right before the Lord is about to genuinely reward you or require a greater level of commitment (whether ministry or otherwise), the enemy approaches you with a very attractive offer? He realizes that you cannot serve God and mammon. That is why discernment is very crucial because not every breakthrough or promotion is from the Lord.

In the wilderness, Satan tempted Jesus. If Satan could not fulfill it, it would not have been a temptation. The Bible declares that Jesus was, indeed, tempted by the devil. The enemy, in a bid to undermine God's purpose, tried to get Jesus to come in at the wrong time. Satan wanted to prematurely expose Jesus to wealth at a time when Jesus was on a mission to redeem this world, not indulge himself and enjoy the riches of this world. Jesus overcame this temptation; and when he rose from the dead, he reconciled all things to Himself, including all the wealth in creation. He waited for the appointed time and took back everything that the devil stole from man. The devil will always try to prematurely expose you to what is already yours, and when you fall for his bait, you eventually miss out on God's best for you.

Unfortunately, some believers settle for this "blessing" at the expense of their own soul. People become enjoined to all kinds of soul ties, get involved in the occult, witchcraft and juju, all for money! The devil's trap of premature exposure to wealth is costly to the victim. What he's tempting you with is already yours in Christ Jesus. "... For all things are yours whether ...things present or things to come; all things are yours; and ye are Christ's and Christ is God's." Don't yield to his "stone", wait for God's appointed time.

"Houses and riches are inherited from parents..." (Prov. 19:14) Every nation, tribe or family has its own system of inheritance and transfer of property from one generation or person to another. Many wealthy parents pass away and bequeath great estates or property to their children and they end up squandering everything, and leaving nothing behind to pass on to the next generation. This is usually a result of children being prematurely exposed to wealth and not being well-trained or brought up to handle material possessions. I have heard many of these sad accounts where the property was sold, and the money spent on drugs, alcohol, women and flamboyant, riotous living.

In Luke 15, we see a related parable told by Jesus:

> There was a man who had two sons. The younger said to his father, "Give me my share of the estate". So he divided his property. Not long after that the younger son got together all that he had and set off for a distant country and there he squandered his wealth in wild living. After he had spent everything, there was severe famine in that whole country and he began to be in need.

We see from the above parable of Jesus that the prodigal son was exposed to wealth at a time when he did not have what it took to handle the inheritance wisely. He had no plan nor did he have a vision. His actions were dictated by money. He wasted everything that was given to him, as is still happening in our day. The prodigal son was fortunate because his father was alive, which made his return home possible. Unfortunately, many inherit from the deceased, which make their return to greatness virtually impossible. Parents need to discern the time to give children their share of an inheritance, so that we don't prematurely expose them to wealth, like the father of the prodigal son did.

No matter how busy we claim to be or how much we strive to leave something of great value behind, we need to realize that investing time to train our children to handle money and material possessions is the most fundamental assurance that what we leave behind will be well managed.

Let's take up this challenge as individuals, as a family and as a nation, to continuously analyze how we are raising our children. We should, always ask ourselves whether we are bringing them up in a way that will enable them to responsibly handle what we are toiling for today. Our children should be able to enjoy a better quality of life than we did. Let's secure their future.

A lot of people get exposed to wealth that leads to their destruction, specifically when it comes in too early. Agur knew this, and that is why he asked God not to bless him so much to the point that he would forget Him. (Prov. 30:7-9). The Bible records that the children of Israel ate and drank and after they were full, rose up to play, which resulted in their destruction (Exodus. 32:6).

And take a close look at this parable Jesus told.

> *And he told them this parable,"… the ground of a certain rich man produced a good crop. He thought to himself, 'What shall I do?' I have no place to store my crops. Then he said, "This is what I'll do, I will*

48

tear down my barns and build bigger ones and there will I store all my grain and my goods. And I will say to myself, 'you have plenty of good things laid up for many years.' Take, live easy and drink and be merry. But God said, "You fool! This very night your life will be demanded of you. (Luke 12:16-26)

This man was so blessed, materially, that there was no room to even store what he had. However, this blessing resulted in his destruction because he made careless utterances.

Every large financial breakthrough you are looking for will test you when it arrives. It will offer you a wider range of choices, new friends and companions, new temptations, new experiences and new troubles. Your ability to enjoy the breakthrough and make the best use of it will be determined by the wise decisions you make, based on your understanding of the purposes for which it was given to you.

Worth mentioning is the desire to enter into business ventures that they have neither proven nor gained insight about, which results in their failure or indebtedness, just because someone is "making it" in a particular business venture does not mean that everyone else will be successful in that same venture. In all your ways, including business ventures, acknowledge God and He shall direct your path. One should gain some amount of experience or associate with someone who has been in that kind of business before entering in. This will ensure that they receive adequate counsel and direction as well as supply them with information and necessary assistance needed to flourish.

In every endeavor or field of life, one needs a mentor, and this also applies to everyone in business. Who is your mentor? Who have you asked to keep you accountable? Who do you speak with to assuage concerns and questions about the manner in which you handle your financial affairs? In business, one needs a mentor who is experienced and has survived the testing and pressures of failure, disappointment, and success. Such people have a lot to offer and just making time to talk with them will bless you and give you practical keys to make it as well.

Unfortunately, we live in an environment where the economic pressure has a tendency to compel one to yield to premature exposure. If one really has a vision to be great, affecting their community, nation and world, then conquering the temptation of premature exposure is a prerequisite.

In Ghana, and most developing countries, potential and talents abound. Unfortunately, these talents are not allowed to mature to the benefit of their people because of the desire to be famous. Through premature exposure, a lot of talents are destroyed or left unexplored. We see it with those in the fields of fashion, music, art, and sports, to name a few. In the Ghanaian sports world, for example, young athletes are hurriedly enticed to play football in Europe.

Most of these athletes are usually young, inexperienced and uninformed about how the "real world" operates. They don't even take into account the different climate in which they are going to be situated. As a result, many soon find themselves ill prepared, cheated, abused and destroyed. If they had been a little patient, and allowed themselves, to be well groomed at home, they would be prepared for the world out there. The National Football League reflects this lapse. The fact that one plays, so well on the junior side doesn't mean they should rush or be rushed to play professionally. They should be encouraged to enhance themselves (i.e. education, obtaining wise counsel, etc.), as well as improve the quality of their game. Let's not forget that every good and perfect gift comes from above not abroad.

A lot of musicians break out on the scene and release powerful albums, only to become history. This is usually a result of premature exposure. Some celebrities cannot handle their premature success, and as a result are disgraced or destroyed in the process.

Remember success does not mean experience. I encourage every one in some form of profession, trade and business to explore the diversity that their field offers. A lot of seamstresses are limited to shirts, trouser, and suits, but I encourage anyone in such a field to adequately prepare themselves and consider the possibility of expanding ones expertise by moving into other areas such as upholstery or possible interior decorating, so that you become a master of your trade. Do not let premature exposure cause you to rush, or rob you of adequate preparation.

If you are working, I encourage you, every now and then, to take refresher courses for perhaps a few weeks (or evening classes). It will help you acquire more skills and also improve your level of operation. Remember that one's level of preparation determines one's impact and accomplishments. Let excellence and being the best, be everyone's goal.

We need to affect our families, our communities, our nations, and ultimately, our world. You can make a difference in your own way. You are not a good steward when you fail to add to or enhance what was originally given to you.   Businesspersons must not neglect their social responsibility. Wait for the appointed time and go through the process. It is the most excellent way because, "...he who gathers money little by little makes it grow..." is the way proverbs puts it.

If all you do as a businessman is provide garbage cans and brooms for keeping your community clean you are making a difference. Do not despise humble beginnings – just watch God bring you from glory to glory.

The acquiring of credit and loans has been a vehicle of premature exposure. Many people bask in the glory of loans and use it to show off instead of using it for its intended purpose. Many also fall into the temptation of posing as if the money they borrowed is not a loan, but their own. It's always better for one to be modest and carefully consider their expenditures until the loan is fully paid.

In the United States, increasing numbers of credit card-debtors end up bankrupt, due to their inability to repay their loans. The exorbitant lifestyles of the 1980's have caught up with many people, and have resulted in families losing their homes, cars and reputations. These individuals are left messed up for the rest of their lives, working only to pay off their debts, because of the premature pleasure the lenient credit systems offer. In short, these loans, when abused, entice you to live today on tomorrow's money.

The effects of premature exposure are not only limited to the individuals involved, but also undermines the economic emancipation and development of nations. When a lot of people within a nation get prematurely exposed to huge sums of money, it usually results in inflation, which is one of the major problems many economies are struggling with today. It also aggravates the balance of payment deficit, which puts the economy in terrible shape.

Premature exposure is characterized by the after-effects of easily accessible loans from international organizations to developing nations, which later results in economic oppression. The vicious cycle of poverty and the insurmountable debt that several developing countries owe to many international creditors attests to this fact. They usually entice these nations to take huge sums of loans, which later gives them the power to hold these debtor nations in economic slavery through the exorbitant interest they exact. It seems then that the poor get poorer and the rich get richer.

A lot of nations are rushing to move into middle-income economies, which is a noble idea. Nevertheless, we ought to be cautious, so we do not destroy our values and sell out everything to the point of allowing foreigners to buy us out of our own nations, in our quest to move into a middle-income economy.

We ought to put structures in place, that will help us fulfill our vision without prostituting our resources and selling our future into slavery, lest we live as slaves in our own land.

Much of the economic collapse and recession hitting Asia and other parts of the world could be attributed to their sudden economic booms. This was coupled with the fact that these nations didn't have the structures and the countermeasures to stabilize the wealth that was accumulated through economic booms. When a nation experiences sudden economic booms, it more often than not has adverse affects on society, as compared to nations that accumulate wealth little by little.

Chapter 5

Premature Exposure to Marriage & Family

Marriage is the union between a man and a woman bonded in a legal and covenant relationship, which makes them husband and wife. God first instituted marriage for Adam and Eve in the Garden of Eden to fulfill His purpose. God provided a helpmeet for Adam to complement him for the fulfillment of His purpose.

Marriage was God's idea. Adam was not consulted when God was forming Eve. Eve was God's surprise to Adam, one that Adam appreciated, accepted and cherished.

If we agree with Scripture that God is the author of marriage, then He's the best specialist to consult concerning issues about marriage. His guidelines must be carefully followed to experience the joy and fulfillment it offers.

According to Dr Myles Munroe, if you want to know the use of a product, you don't ask the product, but the manufacturer. It is time many stopped employing their own strength and wisdom and following solutions that the world is offering. Because God is the author of marriage, we must consult Him for the solutions we are desperately seeking.

Contrary to all the erroneous perspectivespeople have about marriage, it is one of the best things God instituted. He actually saved the best for last!

Marriage is good; Marriage is powerful; Marriage is honorable; Marriage is a mystery. It is a solemn and sacred institution, a serious union that needs to be entered into with all caution, seriousness, and adequate preparation. There are many who take this institution lightly these days and enter into it prematurely. Many make comments like, "Marriage is no big deal it's just one of those things." These will need to know why marriage is sacred, a mystery, a ministry, and a serious union.

Many limit marriage to the wedding ceremony, the feast, and honeymoon. However, those who have been in it for a while will tell a different story. It is a serious union because it binds the husband and wife together in a relationship so close and intimate that their entire future and assignment will be influenced by it. Marriage involves the surrender of self-interest for the benefit of the relationship.

One needs to enter with all caution because an unfulfilled marriage, a struggling relationship, and ultimately divorce are the worst things that could happen to anyone. Many people underestimate the impact of divorce because they fail to recognize the tremendous investment of self that goes into the making of a marriage.

Due consideration is also vital because the mortal man sees on the outside and only God sees what is in the heart and what lies ahead. Everyone needs inside information that will enable one to judge rightly and take the best steps. It does not simply take a man or a woman to make a marriage successful. It takes a loving husband, a caring father, and responsible man to make a marriage work and a virtuous woman, a responsible mother and a good wife to keep it stable.

The Bible says "he that finds a wife finds a good thing and obtains favor from the Lord" (Prov. 18:22). This means that before a woman is found or married, she needs to possess the qualities of a wife. One must recognize that one marries into a family. Family has a strong natural and spiritual influence on anyone. It is believed that if you marry the right person, you have 70% of your problems solved. But, if you marry the wrong person you spend 70% of your time trying to keep the relationship together and have 30% for yourself and other things.

Adequate preparation is crucial because without it, one can be frustrated to the point of backing out. Maturity is an important ingredient that cannot be neglected. Maturity is not just age, but the ability to use the senses to discern right and wrong. Marriage is not for boys and girls, or males and females per se; it goes beyond that. Marriage is for mature men and women.

Marriage is a ministry because the husband and wife ought to minister to each other's material, physical and spiritual needs in a caring, loving, and gentle way. The Bible speaks of the fact that no man hates his own flesh, but he takes cares of it and nourishes it. Men must minister to their wives in the same way. In doing this, the man fulfills the Scripture, because when he loves his wife, he loves himself (Eph 5:28,29). The same applies to physical intimacy. I Corinthians 7:3-5 speaks of not "defrauding" one another, rather the husband and wife should render due benevolence to one another.

Why Satan Hates Marriage

A thriving, successful, honey-filled Christian marriage is one of the greatest threats to Satan and his cohorts. It captures his attention and provokes in him a desire to bring in a wedge or some form of confusion, misunderstanding, and eventually separation. When Adam was alone in the garden, and in control of all the earth, Satan was silent. We never saw Satan until Adam got married to Eve. There was something about the woman and marriage that caused Satan to come out of his hiding place.

Have you ever wondered why your own marriage or that of people around you is always coming under attack? Have you wondered why there is so much confusion, misunderstanding, misinterpretation, provocation, and vexation in many marriages? Have you ever wondered why the divorce and separation rates keep soaring year after year in the world and even in the church? Are you a victim of a broken family or a family on the verge of being broken?

Have you wondered why the problem keeps compounding? Have you wondered why your parents or your friends' parents are always quarrelling and why your neighbor is always abusing his wife? Have you wondered why pastors' marriages come under one of the greatest attacks and their wives or husbands seem to be complaining about their marriage? Have you wondered why a lot of movies now depict adultery as a normal occurrence? The bottom line answer is that Satan doesn't like the institution of marriage, and is attacking it from all angles by whatever means possible. Never in the history of mankind has the institution of marriage come under such attack, criticism, and pressure.

Scriptures about the mystery of marriage will tell you why the enemy is against this noble institution.

Marriage is honourable in all, and the bed undefiled (Heb. 13:4)

Marriage brings honor, and even more when it is pure and untainted by adultery. The devil desires to bring disgrace by attacking marriage.

He who finds a wife, finds a good thing and obtains favor from the Lord. (Prov. 18:22)

The devil doesn't want anybody to find good things and obtain favor in God's sight. The favor of God brings blessings, prosperity, protection and all that undermines Satan's agenda.

Two are better than one (Ecc. 4:9)

One can put on thousand to flight, and two ten thousand (Deut. 13:32)

When a husband and wife are united in prayer or agreement, nothing shall be impossible to them. That is awesome, and too powerful for the devil to handle. This is a serious threat to his kingdom and plans. It therefore causes him to fight and bring situations so there can be no agreement in marriage to disturb his kingdom.

But did He not make them one, having a remnant of the Spirit? And why one? He seeks godly offspring. (Mal. 2:15)

The devil does not want any godly offspring to perpetrate the covenant and the things of God. He wants the earth to be filled with strange and illegitimate children.

I shall build my church and the gates of hell shall not prevail against it (Matt. 16:18)

The Scriptures say that where two or three are gathered in my Name, there I am in their midst. Whenever the husband, wife and family gather in the name of the Lord, God comes into their midst, and the devil cannot stand it. The family is also the first church.

Marriage makes you whole. This doesn't mean that one is not whole before marriage. Jesus, Paul, Daniel, etc were not married, yet they were completely whole people. This means that it makes one complete by surrounding one with assistance. It is only through marriage that one can legitimately fulfill the command to be fruitful and multiply. A lot of people, including myself, will attest that marriage made us better in many ways.

"Marriage is good" and is the climax of God's creation. Marriage can make you the happiest and most fulfilled human being on the earth.

Woe to him that walks alone, if he falls, for he has no one to help him up. (Eccl. 4:10)

The devil wants you walking alone, whether you are married or not. Marriage offers companionship. The devil wants you to walk alone so that when you fall, there is no one to encourage you or lift you up and no one to fan the flame when you are cold.

The devil brings confusion into marriages, making men mistreat their wives and vice versa. When this happens, the prayers of the man are hindered. Satan is unleashing all kinds of terrible assaults to undermine and if possible destroy marriage. He is using a lot of weapons, the most powerful weapon being premature exposure.

The Strategy

The enemy is a long-term planner. He moves into action a long while before his opening. We see from Scripture that he incited King Herod to have all the male boys killed when Jesus was a baby. Pharaoh was inspired by demonic forces to pass a law to kill all the male children at Moses' birth. This was to prevent the child from growing to discover that he was the deliverer of Israel.

The devil has not changed; he does not fight marriage after the husband and wife come together. He employs the more subtle and dangerous weapons of premature exposure to fight their marriage before it takes off. He starts the fight when they are children, or growing up as single people, long before they think about marriage. He does this so that if his plans should work, it becomes more difficult for them to have a fulfilled marriage when the right time comes. Marriage counselors hold that a lot of marital problems have their roots in deep-seeded things that occurred before the marriage.

Sex

Moral authority, purity and fidelity are strong defenses in securing any marriage. Sex before marriage or sex outside marriage is one of Satan's most powerful weapons in his premature exposure arsenal. Satan's targets include adults, youth, little children and generations yet unborn.

Why do you think most best selling books, top draw movies, chart-topping music, and best selling magazines reek with sex? Why do you think that most video rental places in the U.S. have pornography on the top shelves? Why do the most patronized newspapers show nudity? It is a vital part of Satan's major strategy!

If one claims to be a virgin, people look at them funny and ask if there is anything wrong with them. They are teased and called names, and picked on by their peers. Subtly and craftily, they are pressured, directly and indirectly, and made to feel that they are missing something. All these are Satan-orchestrated plots? There is a glory that virginity and moral purity evokes and brings on a person. You are not missing anything if you are a virgin. It is also proof of one's fidelity, chastity, and purity, and I believe that it is the greatest present that one could give their spouse after marriage. If you are pressured, don't give up, because you are on course and doing the right thing.

Moral standards have fallen so drastically that society downplays the consequences of sexual intimacy before and outside of marriage. Society encourages, gives excuses, and makes premarital sex appealing. A lot of young have lost their birthright, destroyed their destinies and complicated their lives through sex before marriage. Many more are on the verge and at risk. Oh, how I pray that you will be delivered and empowered to escape the snare and trap the enemy has laid for you and your loved ones, in Jesus name.

The notion is that, "as long as you feel grown, you can do what you please, only be careful, and get 'protection'." Never forget that the pleasure of sin is but for a moment and sin has its wages. Inflation can change people's wages, but the wages of sin have not changed. It is still death. God has not lowered his standard and does not intend to.

> *The wages of sin is death, but the gift of God is eternal life... (Rom. 6:23)*

The devil, through diverse ways, especially television and Hollywood, has deceived many people, both young and old, that premature pleasure or sex between two unmarried people is not a big deal. Sex is welcomed any time, any place, and with anyone is fine, as long as it gives pleasure, pleasure, and more pleasure.

One more serious thing that a lot of people forget or don't know is that anytime there is sex between a man and a woman, they are making a statement to God, that they are "married". By this act, there is immediately a soul tie that binds them and a covenant is established. The mystery that takes place in marriage takes place during sex. Many say, "I don't love him or her, I am only sleeping with him/her and having a good time". Oh how deceptive! There can be a marriage ceremony, blessing and the feast (reception) but everything is sealed and consummated when the bride and groom get intimate and know each other through sex. Look closely at what the Scriptures say, and you'll understand the mystery that takes place through sex.

> *What? Know ye not that he which is joined with a harlot is one body, for the two saith He shall become one flesh (I Cor. 6:16)*

Here, Paul was talking about fornication and immorality. He was saying that through immorality between two unmarried people or sex with a harlot two people become one flesh. This is serious because many people think that it's over after a sexual encounter, but in actuality they have become connected to their own destruction. It is not over, not at all!

> *Now look at the mystery of marriage. It says at the beginning of creation, God made them male and female. For this reason a man will leave mother and father and the two shall become one flesh (Mark 10:6-8)*

We realize that the mystery of two becoming one flesh takes place when two come together sexually, and when they are joined together by God in marriage. One invokes a blessing and the other a curse and destruction. This is because one glorifies God and the other the devil. Satan hardly changes his strategies. He ties people up in "marriage" in order to frustrate the real marriage at the right time with the right person. Premature exposure through sexual immorality, fornication, adultery, etc. is the root cause of many marital problems.

It is purported that a twinge of guilt over sexual misconduct performed once or many times can later serve as a mental block to sexual enjoyment. Guilt is also a common cause of orgasmic malfunction in many marriages, and this is a serious problem that many marriages are facing and those involved cannot talk about it to anybody because of its sensitive nature. The root of this could be strongly attributed to premature exposure. Sometimes the guilt may be related to an attempted rape for which the unwilling victim feels guilty. It may be incest or abuse by relatives or friends. It may also be an ill-advised adulterous liaison experienced prior to marriage or promiscuity before or after marriage. Guilt is a cruel taskmaster. After such premature pleasures, it must be confronted before one can be free to experience God's best and fulfillment.

Another area that the enemy is using strongly is heavy petting [kissing, fondling, caressing) before marriage. This also carries the power to undermine fulfillment in marriage. Lesbianism is also very dangerous. It is setting many women on the path of being unfulfilled in their marriage and affecting these marriages seriously.

Premature ejaculation for men is also a serious problem in many marriages. It is usually an after effect of those who engage in serious masturbation, homosexuality, pornography, strip tease, and other perverted sexual practices. This is especially prevalent with those who were seriously addicted to it before their marriage. The after effect of this seriously undermines the strength and joy of lovemaking.

There are four levels of maturity, which qualify one to marry. This is basic for adequate preparation. There must be physical maturity, psychological (or mental) maturity, social (which includes material) maturity, and spiritual maturity. The Scripture recalls that "...Jesus grew in wisdom and in stature and in favor with God and man" (Luke 2:52). The term wisdom refers to psychological maturity, stature refers to physical maturity, favor with God refers to spiritual maturity, and favor with man refers to social maturity.

Spiritual Preparation

The spirit realm rules the natural. If you want to prevail in the natural, it must first be secured in the spiritual. This is why adequate spiritual preparation and maturity before marriage is crucial and should be basic to all other preparation.

The Christian's level of spiritual preparation is the basis for true success. Where there is inadequate spiritual preparation, one is prematurely exposing oneself to marriage.

If earthly fathers are consulted for counsel by their children in their choice of a husband or wife, how much more should our Heavenly Father, who is Spirit, be consulted and His approval sought before the marriage proposal.

Why Spiritual Preparation

The wisdom in spiritual preparation is manifold. A lot of broken marriages in our societies and world could have been avoided if there had been much more spiritual preparation before making the decision to marry or enter into those relationships. Don't write a letter and seal it in an envelope and expect the Lord to put his stamp on it! Involve him in the writing of the letter.

We also know That whatsoever the Lord doeth it shall be forever (Eccl. 3:14). Many desire that their marriages and relationships last forever. The key to lasting relationships is spiritual preparation. For one's marital relationship to stand through all tests and trials, one must actively involve God in the initial decision.

On the contrary, if God is left out of our marriage or relationship from the onset and his guidelines and principles not adhered to, we cannot guarantee that the relationship or marriage shall be forever. For when that petite female struts across your office building or a smooth-talking powerful man glances at you, how can you be sure that you will stand? Spiritual preparation is the best guarantee for a successful marriage and meaningful relation-ship.

Whatsoever is born of God overcometh the world (1 John 5:4) If God is the author, your marriage has what it takes to overcome all things. That means you made the Lord the head, seeking Him rightly from the onset for leadership and guidance, following His word faithfully and receiving His blessings, the marriage or relationship will overcome.

When God shuts no one can open and when He opens no one can shut, (Rev 3:7) If God put together a husband and a wife I assure you that no man, woman, devil, situation, or circumstance can put them asunder.

God is very concerned about your marriage and the marriages of all His children. God is a matchmaker and He wants to be part of the choice and decision you make. Nevertheless He leaves the choice of inviting Him with us.

A prudent wife is from the Lord (Prov 19:14b) If one wants a prudent wife he has to receive her from the Lord. He should not make use of his sight because beauty is vain, neither should he use his flesh for the flesh is deceitful. God must provide!

Many people prepare for all other aspects of marriage but do not take spiritual preparation seriously. This is a fatal mistake and a grave misplacement of priorities. Balance is needed in preparation, both naturally and spiritually.

Understanding God's pattern for the family will also reveal the need for spiritual preparation and maturity. God's pattern for marriage and the nuclear family is for the husband to be the head of the woman and for Christ to be the head of the husband (1 Cor. 11:3).

Anytime this order is breached, there will be problems. The man according to God's original plan is supposed to function as the king, the priest, and prophet to his family. If the man is King the wife should be Queen. The man ought to be prepared spiritually. He must be matured enough to function in his role and bring blessings to his family.

The woman also ought to be spiritually mature to submit to the authority God has placed over her. It is very difficult for a woman who is rebellious to the authority God has set over her to submit to her husband. Women who are critical of authority tend to have problems with submission in marriage.

Spiritual preparation is also vital because one marries from a family into a family. When you marry, your spouse's family becomes your family in more ways than one. There may be issues of familiar spirits and strongholds in a spouse's background that may have to be dealt with through prayer, fasting and the word of God before the marriage. Such a background, if not dealt with, can exert strong negative influence on the marriage and family. It may be through the emotions, attitudes or other external influences. Therefore, it is necessary that one is adequately prepared spiritually before marriage, so that one can be in a position to deal with these things.

It may be God's will, yes; it may be flowing with milk and honey, yes; it may be your promised land, yes; but do not forget that there are giants that may have to be conquered. Israel had to fight for their promised land and so must you. With God on your side, you are more than a conqueror. There are certain cases where individuals or tribes are plagued by a curse. It may be certain diseases or cycle of events within the family. In certain families, it could be barrenness, immorality, divorce, separation, drunkenness etc. One should therefore carefully investigate and deal with these so that they and their loved ones do not fall victims to these weaknesses and issues.

Sons usually take after their fathers and daughters after their mothers. There is an old African adage which says, "if you want to have an idea of how beautiful your wife will look in old age look at your mother-in-law." You therefore have to open your eyes and spiritually deal with any thing you may have observed.

One has to ask God for the strategy and power to triumph over things that could undermine the marriage. When one is marrying a man or woman who is not a virgin, especially, those who have had several sexual encounters all the ties need to be broken and the contamination must be cleansed or purged with its consequences reversed as part of the spiritual preparation.

Among some tribes in Ghana, and in many nations around the world, young girls go through all kinds of rites as part of their traditions. Some of these traditions involve the establishment of a blood covenant with the demonic spirit. It has been observed that most of the women from these tribes have serious challenges in their marriages and most marriages end in separation or divorce. Anyone who wants to marry a man or a woman with a similar background should prepare spiritually and deal with that covenant so that the marriage can be secured. It does not matter what you did right or wrong, without spiritual preparation, you are in for a fight, one that could wreck your marriage.

When you have a very precious seed you don't just go and plant it in the bush or a crowded ground. If you do that, you are going to have problems with the seed planted no matter how high its yielding capability and its fruitfulness may be. This seed may have a hard time growing because of the other plants. This is because other plants will be contending with it for nutrients, sunlight, water and so on. The same is true with marriage. Before and after locating your partner there has to be a lot of clearing, uprooting, and burning done in your own life and that of your prospective spouse before planting and watering.

Time after time, there is the need for attention, so that you can yield the best in your relationship. Any time anything springs up it must be carefully pruned or cleared to prevent all forms of encroachment. Every family has its god. If Jesus Christ is not the Lord of the family then even when the person is born again, one has to deal with the spirit that rules the background of the person or it will soon lift itself against the nuclear family and fight the marriage.

If you are marrying into a family in which every marriage ends in divorce or separation or a family in which yours is the first Christian wedding, it is not advisable that one should just go by "faith," without preparing spiritually. It is very risky and dangerous. The enemy must be held at ransom by the power of God's word. The curse of illegitimacy, which usually affects those born out of wedlock and people from polygamous background, must be dealt with.

I have noticed that the enemy takes advantage of these weaknesses to interfere with lots of marriages. You see there are some things which if not dealt with before marriage, may contend with you for the rest of your life. Remember that the moment you marry it becomes difficult to deal with these issues. It is therefore imperative that you deal with them prior to your marriage.

True spiritual preparation before marriage helps a person to die to self. A mark of true spiritual maturity is death to self and loving to death.

The mystery of marriage reveals how crucial spiritual maturity and death to self is. According to the Scriptures it is only when we die that we truly live; and death is the doorway to any miracle. This includes your miracle in marriage. Typologically, the man is God's seed for humanity. Only the seed have the ability to produce after it's kind. Adam was God's grain of seed for the human race; the woman, Eve, came out of him. This is why biologically, the man produces the seed and woman takes and carries the seed from the man during procreation.

In the book of Genesis God said, "the seed of the woman shall bruise the head of the serpent" (Gen 3:15). The seed was a man – Christ Jesus, Gal 3:16; 4:4). It was a miracle because women, naturally, do not produce seed. To rectify humanity's problem, God introduced Christ as the second seed.

Jesus said 'except a grain of seed fall to the ground and dies it abides alone (John 12:24). This presupposes that falling to the ground and dying is the only process that a grain of seed goes through to prevent it from being alone. So we realize that when Adam was single and alone in the garden, God applied the principle Jesus spoke of above for the creation of the woman, which changed Adam's status from being single or alone.

And God said it was not good for the man to be alone. I will make a helper suitable for him so the Lord caused the man (the seed) to fall into a deep sleep and open his side and took a rib to form eve and closed up his side again (Gen. 2:21). One can therefore say that falling into a deep sleep (symbolic of being dead) was what Adam had to undergo to have his wife Eve. God gave him a wife, a skillfully crafted partner to assist and complement him. This is the one that made multiplication possible. If you are willing to follow the principle and allow it to work in you God will give you a perfect wife also.

The second Adam (Jesus Christ) had to die on the cross and after he died, his side was pierced and when he rose from the dead, God gave him a glorious bride – the church. To be able to have a glorious bride or a successful marriage, one has to die to self. If God used this for Adam and Jesus his son whom he loved to give them their brides respectively, then to die to self qualifies one for marriage.

You have to come to a place where you have prepared yourself to die in order to live. Not the same life you led before your "death" but a glorious one after your resurrection. This is why scripture admonishes husbands to love their wives as Christ loved the church and laid down his life for the church.

If one wants to be a husband, one of the main things that qualify him is the ability to die for his wife. Therefore, if one wants to be a husband but is unwilling to die for his wife, he is prematurely exposing himself. In the sight of man, he may be qualified but because he does not possess the spiritual maturity and love to be a husband he does not qualify in the sight of God.

If every woman marries a husband that is willing to die to himself in order to obtain her, what a better society and family the world will witness. Dare to make a difference by being that kind of husband. And dare to be the woman that will marry such a person.

Marriage will stretch you to the limit, and unless you are "dead", you will find reason to back out. The books you read or the tapes you have listened to may not carry you, for there are some things only experience can teach. Sometimes you will feel like you married a person different from the one you thought you vowed to at the altar. There are many times in marriage when one has to die to one's opinions personal comfort, pride and even be like a fool for the sake of love and peace.

The reason why a lot of handsome men and beautiful women cannot keep a successful marriage is because they cannot die to self. Things sometimes happen in marriage that could literally kill you, all the same you need love to help you hang on and endure because it makes you a better person. As I previously stated, there are many times in marriage when one has to die to one's opinions, personal comfort, pride and even be like a fool for the sake of love and peace.

After the affliction you shall see the light. It sometimes takes people who are dead to stomach certain things and adjust to all the differences and still join together to fulfill God's purpose for marriage. You cannot kill an already dead person that is why you need to die to self before marriage so that nothing can kill you in your marriage. Prepare yourself spiritually.
It is through spiritual preparation and spiritual exercises that you mortify deeds of the flesh. Crucify it so that God will be glorified in your marriage.

Physical Preparation

Physical preparation or maturity is very necessary. In certain countries the minimum age is set by the constitution. In Ghana the set age is 18. Sex between boys and girls is prohibited in many cultures and religions around the world. As a matter of fact, even those who are married out young are not allowed to have sexual relations until they come to a certain age. The importance of physical maturity can be defended in many traditional cultures. Various rites and customs of physical maturity are performed in order to gauge the maturity of one who desires to move from childhood to adulthood.

This same principle is demonstrated in Scripture. Physical maturity is necessary in marriage. This is why God, in all his wisdom, said that marriage must be for men and women, not for boys and girls. A man is simply an adult male and a boy is a young male. Similarly a woman is simply an adult female and a girl is a young female.

The spiritual man goes beyond the dictionary definition. In the scriptures a man is an adult male that is physically, socially and spiritually mature or well developed; that is, one who can shoulder responsibility. The scripture did not use "boy" but man. If God instituted marriage for man then physical maturity comes to play. Again we see from the scriptures that in the beginning of creation God made them male and female. "For this reason a man will leave father and mother and be united to his wife and the two will become one flesh, so they are no longer two but one."

Leaving one's father and mother denotes detachments, a crossing over from a life of dependence to a life of independence. A life of independence involves the ability to shoulder responsibility and make wise decisions independently. You cannot marry and still be dependant. This is why a man should be gainfully employed before marriage to enable him, take care of his wife and family. Paul said that since there is so much immorality each man, not a boy, should have his own wife and each woman, not girl, her own husband.

A mature son takes a lot of things into consideration before making a marriage decision. Decision-making is directly influenced by ones level of cognitive development. Therefore, it is crucial that one matures enough to the status of a man or woman, one with the ability to handle responsibility independently before marrying. This will help the young ones avoid premature exposures in marriage.

Maturity is also necessary biologically for women to avoid childbirth complications during delivery. For women, physical stamina is vital to cope with the rigors of marriage, especially in Africa and in developing nations. Observations indicate that between 15-19 years of age, what is usually referred to, as "love" could be mere infatuation.

Financial Preparation

Likening marriage to the human body, one can say that love is the heart; understanding is the head; and money is the backbone. Love undisputedly plays the most important role in marriage, but the very nature of love is shown in giving. This makes it very important for one to be financially prepared before marrying. It is not enough to say you love somebody and go ahead and marry him or her without adequate financial preparation. This is not only unacceptable and unwise, it is also very dangerous, unscriptural, and out of order. One needs to be prepared financially because love is not just words, the I-love-you and the romantic talk is not sufficient to hold a marriage together. Love is an act!

In marriage it is the responsibility of the man to provide for the family. It takes money to put food on the table, to provide clothes and shelter for the family and to pay bills. There are three major things that influence every marriage, communication, sex, and money. This demands that one should be adequately prepared. Love alone does not answer everything; but money does (Eccl. 10:19).

One of the questions I usually ask young men and people who come to see me about getting married is, "Do you have a job?" "Do you earn enough to take care of a wife?" Enough to take care of a family? Some marry by faith without adequate preparation and careful planning. The Bible says, to your faith, add wisdom (2Peter 1:5-7).

For those who seem not to understand me on this point I would like them to answer this question. Will you marry off your daughter in whom you have invested so much over the years to somebody who is not working and is financially unstable? To a man who wants to marry just by faith? Money is not everything; but it is undoubtedly important. If love is true, then it must wait; for love is patient. Many hold that love is blind; however, love should not lose sight of common sense! To enter into marriage one must have a job and a reliable source of income. A source that allows one to budget, plan, pay bills and feed the family.

But if any provide not for his own, and especially for those of his own house, he hath denied the faith, and is worse than an infidel (1Tim 5:8)

According to the Scripture, whoever calls himself a Christian, and is not able to take care of his family is said to be worse than an infidel or an unbeliever. Again, one must not only have a source of income, but must also have the wisdom to manage money.

Money must also serve its purpose so that it does not take the place of God. Any man who does not pay his tithe faithfully is not financially prepared for marriage. This is because such a person comes under a financial curse; one who blocks the blessings of his family and denies them financial freedom. This applies to women as well. Every good wife should be prepared financially, so she'll be able to manage what her husband provides for the house. Because life is filled with surprises, preparation becomes important.

House and riches [are] the inheritance of fathers: and a prudent wife [is] from the LORD. (Proverbs 19:14)

She seeketh wool, and flax, and worketh willingly with her hands. She considereth a field, and buyeth it: with the fruit of her hands she planteth a vineyard. She perceiveth that her merchandise [is] good: her candle goeth not out by night. She maketh fine linen, and selleth [it]; and delivereth girdles unto the merchant. (Prov. 31:13,16,18,24)

The virtuous woman, who is a perfect model for every wife, offers insight for financial preparation. She is portrayed as one who is financially stable. She knows how to manage money and invest properly with a sense of financial discipline. Such qualities do not spring up overnight. One must be trained to have such qualities. Do not marry on borrowed money. It puts you through unnecessary pressure, which sometimes results in quarrels and other unnecessary trouble. It also undermines your manhood. As a man, you should not allow the woman to pay for everything, neither should the woman allow the man to pay for everything. Each partner should contribute his or her part.

Most of the time there is a tendency to borrow one's way out. The beginning of every thing is important, and it is not wise to borrow money to start your marriage. It is premature. Take your time, work hard, save enough, and trust God for favor to be able to handle it. If you cannot afford a Saturday wedding, with all the costs, then get married on a Sunday. You can have a small reception for close relatives and loved ones. You can use the money to do something productive rather than wallow in debt. I am not saying that you cannot love without money; I am saying that entering marriage without money is treacherous!

Psychological Maturity

It is very important for one to be psychologically mature before marriage. This helps sustain the marriage and empowers the couple to fulfill their vision as husband and wife. It is also an invaluable asset in building a successful home. Psychological maturity involves ones cognitive development as well as ones emotional development. This will ensure that ones conduct in marriage is not egoistic but altruistic. This level of maturity is the kind that makes one knowledgeable and equips one with the wisdom that only experience brings. The understanding of a child differs from that of a mature person.

This is what Apostle Paul was talking about in 1 Cor. 13:11, " When I was a child I spoke as a child understood as a child, I thought as child but when I became a man I put away childish things." Marriage is not for children; so childish things must be put away. The bible enjoins men to dwell with women according to knowledge (1 Pet. 3:7). This knowledge is not only intellectual, but also experiential.

Men and women need knowledge about each other. Men need to learn how to communicate with women, how they feel, how they interpret events and so on. Women need to also learn what is important to men, understand their needs and relate accordingly. A lack of this knowledge may be detrimental to the relationship. Ones level of cognitive or mental development determines how one thinks, understands, and speaks. Children tend to more egoistic, narrow minded, as well as feeble-minded. They tend to look at things from their own perspective and not give much attention to that of others. The mature are more altruistic, strong-willed and usually forthright in thinking.

Love, which is the heart of every marriage, is not egoistic but altruistic demonstrating that marriage is for the mature. "Charity [Love] suffereth long is kind charity envieth not charity vaunteth not itself is not puffed up doth not behave itself unseemingly , seeketh not her own is not easily provoked , thinketh no evil rejoiceth not in iniquity but rejoiceth in truth. Beareth all things believeth all things hopeth all things indureth all things," (1 Cor 13:4-7). These qualities are clearly not for the shallow minded but for those with deep understanding and wisdom. Emotionally one has to know through wisdom and by virtue of their maturity when to express or suppress emotions.

In other words, self-control is a characteristic of a mature person. One must not allow his emotions to rule his reasoning but rather allow his reasoning to rule his emotions. Your ability to subject your thoughts and feelings to your rationale depends on your level of maturity. What you say or do in marriage is very important as it makes or breaks the marriage. That is why you have to be matured enough to communicate appropriately. The role knowledge and wisdom play in marriage in connection with ones psychological maturity cannot be overemphasized. Many marriages have broken up as a result of misunderstandings that maturity could have recognized.

Chapter 6

Premature Exposure to Christian Leadership

Premature exposure in Christian leadership is not uncommon. Many of the conflicts, church splits, disunity, misunderstanding and carnality we see in the Christian leadership circles can mostly be attributed to premature exposure.

This happens because the price that had to be paid during preparation to offer quality and mature leadership was not fully paid. Many of these ill-prepared leaders easily fall prey to the enemy and his schemes because they have a weak foundation of the faith. Few can soundly teach congregations the true meaning of salvation, the cross, the blood of Jesus, justification, sanctification and other doctrines of the Christian Faith. Many also do not know the ways of God. Anything that is not well prepared poses a threat to the Body of Christ and more so when people receive it without question.

God usually picks people from nowhere and takes them somewhere. He picks a "nobody" and makes him a "somebody." As a result many are tempted to think that they have arrived, especially when they are coming from "nowhere". This is not supposed to be so, we need to acknowledge where we come from and where we are going, so that we do not settle for anything or get puffed up.

This is why Paul the apostle said, "for ye see your calling brethren, how that not many wise men after the flesh, not many mighty, not many noble are called. But God has chosen the foolish things of this world to confound the wise and God has chosen the weak things of this world to confound the things, which are mighty. And the base things of this world are the things which are despised hadn't God chosen, yea and the things that are." (1 Cor. 1:26-28)

The above scripture reveals what we were and what stuff we were made of before God called us. God uses the foolish things, base things, weak things and things that are despised. According to Scripture, this is our nature. If we acknowledge that God's word is true and is applicable to us, we never have to entertain the idea that we can make it on our own or ever take decisions independent of God and expect to succeed.

It is He who makes us. He said, "follow me and I will make you fishers of men" (Matt. 4:19). If we are ever to have significant impact for God, we must allow him to make us, promote us, instruct us, and lead us. Without his leading all our efforts and successes are with no real meaning or lasting significance.

Every building, ministry, church and good Christian stands on a foundation. It is the foundation that determines the height, size, and strength of a building. The body of Christ stands on a foundation of the apostles and prophets with Jesus Christ being the cornerstone of the foundation.

It is unfortunate to see people rush to build ministries and expose themselves when they have not laid a solid or firm foundation. There are a lot of people who profess to be Christians who haven't been through foundational classes and who do not know the basic foundational truths of the Christian faith. Some never went for the classes while others started and never finished. Yet some of such people are in leadership positions by virtue of their spiritual gifts, talents, and placement in society, wealth and so on.

These people may be elders, deacons, board members, musicians, pastors, Sunday school or children's teachers, prophets etc. This is premature exposure and can be detrimental to the individual in the long run. Your preparation is your foundation for leadership. Your service is also a way of building a solid foundation.

The foundation is the hidden part of the building or ministry. It includes those things for which there seems to be no apparent reward. However, these are things that sharpen your character, build you up, helps your inner man, and equip you with knowledge, experience and information. These are the experiences that prune, chastise and stabilize you.

Your preparation is the foundation for the fulfillment of your assignment. Take time to build and work on your foundation. Many who have fallen look back and wish they had taken more time to prepare. Jesus shared the parable of the wise and foolish builder to help us to understand the importance of sound and solid foundations.

> *Therefore everyone who hears these words of mine and puts them into practice is like a wise man who built his house on the rock. The rains came down, the storms rose and the winds blew. And beat against the house; yet it did not fall, because it had its foundation on the rock. But everyone who hears these words of mine and does not put it them into practice is like a foolish man who built his house on sand. The rain came down, the streams rose, and the winds blew and beat against that house and it fell with a great crash. (Matt 7:24 27)*

Now with the two builders the problem was not the flood, nor winds nor rains or even the "beating against" it was the foundation. One did not take time to go through the right process of building. The account in Luke 6: 47-49 even puts it more vividly: it describes the man as one "building his house that dug deep and laid the foundation on the rock". But of the foolish man, He said, he "built the house on the ground without a foundation".

I believe the foolish man was in a hurry to prove a point and make a statement. He could even have mocked or made others mock the wise builder for taking a long time to build the foundation. He forgot that life has many seasons and elements of testing. If there is a weak foundation a downfall is sure.

The floods and the streams generally represent attacks of the enemy. For when the enemy comes in like a flood the Spirit of the Lord will raise up a standard against him. In Revelation 12:15, the serpent spewed water like a flood against the woman and the child. Anything that glorifies God or blesses humanity is an affront to the enemy and therefore subject to demonic attack. However, the attack will not prevail if the foundations are strong and solid.

Winds usually represent change. There are always changes in life. No condition is permanent. There will definitely be changes and God uses these to establish and give one depth. God wants us in a place where we can stand through the storms, a place where our feet shall be planted. Without a solid foundation changes will ruin us and everything else we have built.

Many backslide as a result of a change in location. This happens due to a weakness in the foundation. Changes are not meant to cause you to backslide. On the contrary, they are designed to help deepen your roots and mature you in the things of God.

The rains, which signify the blessings of God, will also come. Temporary success may be gained here and there. Success or blessings can also destroy a man if he is not been prepared to handle them. Do not be in too much of a hurry to be successful and famous.

Success and blessing will test your love and commitment to God in ways that will astound you. Success has destroyed many ministers. Such Pastors find it hard to take advice or relate to their pastors and workers. Some also find it difficult to walk in humility while staying focused on their God given assignment. The season for rains will come but if you have understanding of divine timing and your foundation is strong, you will be able to stand and make the best of all the rains, floods and winds.

Do not allow premature exposure to deny you the wonderful privilege of studying the word and building a firm foundation. Remember many are called, few are chosen and even fewer are faithful to the end. It is not enough to be only called; one must prove faithful and consistent between the calling and the election.

God is against premature exposure in Christian leadership. His word is explicitly clear that a novice should not be put in an office. (1 Tim. 3:6) Christian ministry cannot and must not be taken lightly. Things cannot be done leisurely, because God is holy and the things that have to do with Him must be done with the Divine Standard in mind. He is also a God of specifics who has set rules, standards and procedures through which one can qualify for Christian Leadership. The minister is the shepherd who stands as God's mouthpiece to the people. Many leaders do not understand the importance and significance of this position.

To gain deeper understanding, let us travel to the origin of the priesthood as this depicts the way God selects, prepares and equips human beings to stand before him to minister to him and his people.

The Priesthood

The office of the priesthood was originally intended for the house of Aaron and his descendants. Aaron was the first high priest of Israel and his tribes, Levi, produced the Priests and Levites who ministered with him.

In Exodus 27, God instructed Moses to set aside and consecrate Aaron and his sons to minister unto Him. He had special garments made for them. There were the inner garments, outer garments and the ephod. They could not just go before God in whatever way they chose. They had to dress the way God wanted and required. They had to look different. These garments had connotations and meanings, which are relevant for our understanding and application.

There are different levels and realms in God. In the tabernacle there was the outer court, which had the holy place and holy of holies. If you wanted to access the holiest place, you had to be well dressed and well prepared. It took a certain person with a certain dress, to get a certain place. Those who tried to rush through were destroyed. But even before they were dressed to minister, God required that they washed their hands and feet [Ex 29:4].

Many have died in ministry because they failed to follow God's prescribed pattern. In the Old Testament death was immediate and many corpses were pulled out of the tabernacle. However, in the New Testament grace is available yet this grace is not to be taken advantage of.

The New Testament minister carries out his duties with his hands. The hands are laid on the sick and used to anoint. It is the hands that are used for impartation, commission and ordination. It is also the hands that are lifted in blessing and worship. Thus God requires that through the worship, and the water of the word, one is thoroughly cleansed and placed in the position to minister. God wants hands that worship and serve Him to be holy.

All the numerous stages that the Old Testament priest went through were preparatory. They needed to take time to build up discipline and knowledge. It really disturbs me to imagine how a person who preaches to God's people can do so having not read through the Bible, from Genesis to Revelation, even once. How can you teach somebody from a textbook that you have not fully read?

There are three stages in ministry, the calling, consecration and commissioning or ordination. The Calling makes you aware of God's role in ministry. The Consecration draws attention to your own personality in ministry. The Commissioning declares you to the people over whom God has made you a shepherd. They are all stages that take time, and every minister must go through them.

The man of God should not do things anyhow. He must be aware of his unique responsibilities and prepare adequately to handle them. Even in prayer, I want you to know that different levels exist, which further depict higher responsibility. Asking is the basic level for children. Seeking which takes a lot of effort and energy is the focus of another level. The next level, knocking, takes much force, persistence, and endurance.

Again, understand that what you feed on determines how far you are able to go. We know that milk is for babes. One cannot try to eat meat when he has not finished taking his milk. Sometimes people who are still on milk try to take the meat of the leadership. One cannot run when he has not learnt to crawl or walk. The seven sons of Sceva tried to eat meat while they were still on milk and ended up in trouble. The "evil spirits" chased them and they fled almost naked. (Acts 19:14, 15)

Many ministers preach all kinds of things from the altar of the Lord. They have also allowed untrained people to preach heresies from their pulpits. Offering anything unclean on the altar, in the Old Testament, attracted seven punishments from God. It could cost one's life, blessing and other good things. It always incurred God's wrath and judgment.

Christian leadership is something that is unique in that it does not take one's own might or power but total and absolute dependence on the Spirit of God. "It is not by might, not by power but it's by my spirit saith the Lord of hosts" (Zech. 4:6). This makes it imperative for every Christian leader to walk in step with the Spirit and not their own pace. What a lot of leaders forget is the admonition of Jesus that "without me you can do nothing" (John 15:5). Many ministries are doing things that appear fruitful on the outside but yield nothing.

Jesus said he is the vine and we are the branches (John 15:1). Remaining in Jesus is the key to bearing fruit. For in all your ways, you are to acknowledge him. The reason why people are not bearing fruit that abides forever is that they have gone their own way. They are employing their own strategies to bear fruits other than what Jesus has purposed for them. Jesus taught, "Whatsoever has not been planted by my father shall be rooted out". So shall their fruit be.

Friend, if you have established something by your own might for your own pleasure, be ready to see it uprooted and allow the Lord to lead you in the path that He wants you to walk in.

Lets not forget that we have been called to serve and not to please ourselves. We only present that which the Master wants. If he does not want something, forget it and quit trying to force it.

God instructed Moses, "see to it that you build according to the pattern that I showed you on the mountain." (Exod 25:9) God would not accept anything less or more. A lot of people are building ministries by their own leading, what they think, what others are doing and so on.

However, all such people are in for a shock, because God has to destroy the wrong things in order to begin the right things. For He declared, "I will build my church."

When we act according to our own leading, we should not be surprised when the onslaught of hell starts devastating everything we build. Religion is not what God is asking for. He is seeking an intimate relationship with you. As a bride and a groom, born out of love, deep reverence and total submission and with full trust. Much religious activity in the church today is merely the fleshly, characterized by busyness supposedly "for the Lord." This includes evangelism, building projects, prayer meetings, teaching, school activity and many others, yet so little is achieved despite the effort being put in.

Leaders and church folks who do not allow themselves to be led by God and guided by the Holy Spirit will surely reap decay, and destruction. Many Christian leaders decide who to marry, where to marry, how to run their church, what to teach their church members, who to help with counseling, and so on. Instead they should ask the Holy Spirit to show them what to do and allow Him to run the show. In this way, life is released into the leader and the congregation. Many have been called and chosen by God yet premature exposure is luring them into wasting God's resources, destroying God's heritage and deviating from God's plan for their lives.

Are you using God's resources, as he will have you to? How do you draw your budget? If you want success, be led by the spirit of God and do not depend on your own strength. Many people rush into ministry because they think they are ready. Well, it is not what you think, it is what He says; otherwise you sent yourself, He did not send you. God never sends people He didn't prepare and He will never ask you to do something that He hasn't equipped you to do.

Jesus emphatically commanded His disciples, "Tarry ye in Jerusalem till ye be endued with power from on high" (Luke 24:49). If they had gone before then, they would have prematurely exposed themselves. They would also have missed God's timing during the outpouring and wouldn't have had success like they did.

Lets not forget that these disciples had to wait before going to preach the gospel. Tarry denotes waiting, tarry means stay for a while. It develops patience, which is vital for every proper preparation. It involves long suffering and endurance. "Tarry ye", He said to them.

Now these disciples had walked with Jesus in so close a relationship for about three and a half years, they saw him, ate together, slept together, preached together, cast out devils and came back with testimonies. They did everything with Jesus. They had a lot to offer but according to God's perfect will, they were not ready. They saw Him crucified, buried and raised from the dead and yet He told them to wait a while.

What is it that makes some leaders so confident that they believe they know everything? What makes them so confident that they see no need to wait for His directives and mandate to go? What encounter have you had so far and what have you done that makes you feel you can go on your own? Without waiting, seeking his face, listening to his voice and knowing his perfect will?

What should make one feel so ready? The only thing that qualifies you to go is if He says, "go" not when somebody says or you think it's time or circumstances or experiences say so. Jesus told them to tarry because there is always something beyond your imagination that God especially has in store for you. He is getting ready to unleash you like a mighty weapon [Jer. 51:20].

God has miracles for you, which you have not seen before. As the disciples tarried they were filled, baptized, gifted and endued with supernatural power and they became mighty world shaking witnesses. Not a shameful, frustrated, confused and confounded witness but a powerful force.

The secret of being filled with the Holy Ghost and being endued with power from on high is tarrying. It is my prayer that you will wait for God's timing so that signs and wonders will follow you. There are a lot of people who claim they have been sent who have not been sent, they have simply commissioned themselves.

Many do not even know the specific area of their call. Many also run with the other people's messages. This is not supposed to be so. You have to run with the message that God has given you. Everyone that God called, prepared and commissioned was given a particular message with a specific mission. In other words those who are called have a job description and assignment.

There are many pastors who do not have fathers or big brothers to whom they are accountable. These are "lone rangers" doing their own thing. Many of these people spend time with peers and friends who cannot correct, advise or rebuke them. Any person who falls into the above category has prematurely exposed himself or herself.

How can one be a good shepherd or leader if he has not been led? He will abuse all the people he leads because he has not been led before. Only good shepherds can lead sheep to the right place and take good care of the flock. Lets therefore follow after Jesus, the Good Shepherd, in His example of submissiveness and humility.

Leaders must realize that in God's eyes people are priceless. He became a man, lived among man and died a horrid death on Calvary, all for the love of people. Because God takes people seriously, those in Christian leadership must take their role just as seriously. Leaders must remember that God is in the people business and that if they accept the call they need to prepare themselves adequately.

Much of today's Christian leadership resembles corporate America. It is characterized by competition, selfish ambition and greed. Leaders must be aware that all their service is designed to bring glory to God not to themselves. Leaders must be aware that they do not know all things and must be willing to be corrected. It is when leaders become prideful that they fall. If you are a Christian leader, please remember that you are in this business for souls and things of eternal significance. Take time to prepare yourself and allow the Lord to break and make you.

When asked what he would do differently in ministry, a well-known pastor with 50 years of experience in ministry simply said, "I would take less speaking engagements and study more." Ministry is not simply standing on a pulpit and telling the masses what they need to do, it is taking care of people, feeding them the right things, respecting them enough to say you're sorry when you make a mistake, loving them when it hurts and so on.

Many people prematurely expose themselves to ministry because they have a mistaken view of what ministry is. Take time to prepare yourself for there is more at stake than your reputation and financial position; there are souls on the line! May the Lord bless you as you take care of His most prized possession.

Chapter 7

Indicators of Premature Exposure

It has been said that prevention is better than cure and the best form of defense is offense. The world is striving hard and taking measures to safeguard themselves against things they dread. Immunization is one of the medical methods employed to prevent people from falling prey to disease and illness while also building their immune system.

This information is designed to equip you with divine immunity as well as provide you with clues to discern whether an exposure in life is premature or not. One can also determine whether or not where they currently find themselves is a result of premature exposure, and what approach to employ in dealing with their situation.

Regardless of what we think or perceive of opportunity, it must align itself with divine timing and God's designated process. There is the good and acceptable will, the permissive will, and the perfect will of God. What we are talking about is walking in the perfect will of God.

A classic example is the act of sex. Sex is a powerful creation of God, which is good and it is meant to be experienced between a man and a woman who are bonded legally and publicly in the covenant of marriage, as husband and wife. It is a demonstration of their love, commitment and affection for each other. However, this same act, at the wrong time with the wrong person can be fornication, rape, adultery, or incest, and thus incur the anger of its victims, those related to them, the general public, the law, but more seriously, the wrath and judgment of God.

With fornication, for instance, the grounds for it being wrong, is the inappropriate timing of the sexual act. This includes those who have a few weeks before they tie the knot! The timing is right and mature only after the marriage ceremony. Any act of sexual intercourse that happens before marriage is a premature exposure to sex, which has serious consequences.

Unorthodox Means

One indicator, which can be used to detect premature exposure, is when one has to employ unorthodox means to get things done. Unorthodox refers to neglecting stipulated methods or abusing the legal process. Many people usually resort to lying, slandering, backbiting, defrauding, manipulating, scheming, shedding innocent blood, cheating and a host of endless, unethical vices to attain some things.

As a Bishop, I have come across many that have been trapped in this web, especially those in ministry. Some employed unorthodox means and strategies to start their ministries. They, at a point, seemed to be gaining credible success, until the tables were turned and they began to reap what they had sown. This is a principle that cannot be repeated enough times.

Charisma and the anointing are very powerful and can bring one into prominence in ministry, business, politics and other fields of human endeavor. However, it takes character not only to get to the top but also to remain at the top.

Employing unorthodox means like lying, cheating, and using destructive criticisms against others in ministry to gain success or favor instead of praying, loving, or correction in the spirit of love and humility makes ones success short-lived. The reason the success is short-lived is simple. There is always a time of testing for every relationship, vision, dream, course, and ministry. Unfortunately, because the ministry was prematurely exposed, it will fall into serious jeopardy or even be destroyed.

Secondly, employing unorthodox means exposes the ministry prematurely to the assaults of principalities and satanic powers that the ministry has not developed the required spiritual capacity and endurance to handle.

If you claim to be a heavyweight, the opponents assigned to you are heavyweights. Woe unto you if you don't belong in the heavyweight division, and God is not on your side because you have gone your own way instead of His!

Jesus Christ was faced in the wilderness and tempted by Satan. It was a "god-level battle". It must be realized that it wasn't just any principality or demon or power that came against Jesus, but it was Satan himself, in his capacity as the god of this world to contest Jesus, the Son of God.

To buttress the above, we realize from the account of Jesus' temptation that the first thing Satan said to him was "If you are the son of God ...", which he repeated in the next temptation, signifying that he was questioning Jesus' Sonship and dealing with him at that level. In the final temptation, Satan came out as the god of this world when he said, "All this power will I give thee and the glory of them, for it is delivered unto me and whosoever I will I give it. If thou therefore will worship me all shall be thine." (Matt. 4:4-8)

Many lack this understanding that there are levels and ranks. This is why some ministries have collapsed and many are struggling without making any progress. In frustration many refer to their call and come out with justifiable evidence to attest to their calling. However, a careful look at the process employed reveals Satan's foothold. Whenever you employ unorthodox means or a medium contrary to God's stipulated process, you begin to force your way to make things happen resulting in terrible consequences.

Employing unorthodox means is a blatant sign of lack of faith in God's ability to accomplish what you intend to perform. It is also a sign of impatience and a lack of spiritual stamina to wait and absolutely depend on God to fulfill His promise. Whatever God has purposed shall stand and what God has spoken, He will bring it to pass (Isa. 14:24). God will not use unorthodox means to bring His plans to pass. His way is perfect and He makes all things beautiful in His time (Eccl. 3:11).

If you have to employ dubious means to attain an end, beware you may be prematurely exposing yourself by going ahead of God. In ministry there is a lot of pressure to "make it", get famous, or bring you to people or situations that you are not ready for. Jesus said, "If they did it to me they will do it to you for the servant is not greater than his master (John 13:16). If the devil tempted Jesus by asking him to stand at the highest point of Jerusalem and throw himself down to gain popularity and show his might, then he will surely tempt every minister to employ unorthodox means to reach their end.

When it comes to using unorthodox means one can quote seemingly justifiable scriptures like the devil did. We must follow the leadings of the Holy Spirit in righteousness and not the letter only.

In the business world, it is much more prevalent for people to recommend the employment of unorthodox means. They maintain that it is the nature of the system, the normal way to make it. But let' s not forget that God has commanded that "...thou shall not steal", "thou shalt not swear falsely..." and "...a false balance is an abomination unto Him". We are supposed to be the salt of the earth and the light of the world (Matt 5:13-14).

Success that comes through dubious means brings premature exposure. Remember that it is only a trap to ensnare and destroy the business and all one can have in the future. Do not yield to unorthodox means for it is better to gain little by little and have God, Who is your fulfillment and sufficiency than to have abundance without Him, only to lose it eventually (Prov. 15:16)

This is the same in marriage, where many are employing all kinds of unorthodox means like snatching people's husbands and wives from them. Many also employ juju, voodoo, consult spiritualists, and messengers of Satan to help them seduce and entice people to marry them. Some have used lies, sex, threats, and blackmail to trap a partner.

When people find themselves applying these unorthodox principles, they are prematurely exposing themselves and failing to wait for God's timing. If you have already entered into marriage through these means, you need to repent and rectify the situation, which will be discussed in detail in the final chapter.

In the arena of politics, using unorthodox means to gain political power is an indication of premature exposure. An example of this was Hazel, king of Aram. The servant of God, Elisha, told Hazel that he would be the next king. He had been sent by King Ben-Hadad to inquire from the prophet Elisha, whether he would recover from his sickness. Upon returning, having heard the prophecy of his kingship, he killed King Ben-Hadad in his bed the next day by putting a wet blanket to his face, and assuming the throne immediately, (2 Kings 8:7-11). This was unlike David who did not shed Saul's blood but waited patiently for his time.

Therefore, having to employ unorthodox means is a major indicator of premature exposure from God's perspective. And this is so when those involved are divinely destined for what they prematurely run after.

The Peace of God

Life is full of choices. People make decisions everyday. They may be trivial or major such as receiving a job offer, which may be of strategic importance or a change of career.

Man is a spirit with a mind, living in a body. With your body, you deal with the physical world; with your mind you deal with the social and intellectual world; and with the spirit, you deal with the spiritual realm. God is Spirit, and because of that he usually communes with our spirit. As He communes with us, we receive promptings in our spirit and receive impressions, which cannot be easily expressed because they are independent of what we see.

For every person, especially those who have a relationship with God, and maintain constant fellowship, their spirit becomes sensitive and receives promptings and signals. This is not limited exclusively to those who are saved, but it also happens in the lives of unbelievers. In the case of unbelievers, such encounters tend to lead them to Christ.

There are several instances in which people share testimonies and say "something told me or I felt very strongly." You may even have had this experience before. That "something" is usually the Holy Spirit prompting or sending signals to your spirit to alert you or lead you in a particular direction. Usually, obedience to that prompting may result in a deliverance, success, joy, or peace on the inside even though there may be nothing on the outside.

Therefore, one way of checking if an exposure or offer is of God or premature is by being still and checking from within your heart, whether you have the peace of God concerning the situation. When there is that peace within, there is a high probability that it is of God and the timing is right. On the contrary, when everything appears well on the outside while your spirit feels agitated, it may be an indication that something is not right and that the exposure is premature. The best thing to do is to take some time to ask God to show you why you are feeling that unrest. He will reveal the reason to you.

Many times, your spirit may be warring with your soul concerning an issue that takes away your peace on the inside. Whenever your emotions, mind, circumstances and your senses are all crying for a particular thing, while deep inside there is a nudging; I admonish you to obey your spirit.

A lot of people ask, "Bishop, is it possible to sense the peace of God in times of trouble, even when everything around you seems to be against you?" My answer, from personal experience is, "Yes, you can." Because He is your very present help in the time of trouble, and He is the Prince of Peace, whenever He is around you there is peace. The experience of peace is a strong pointer that the timing for you is divine and the presence of God is with you to make things better.

Will it Endanger You and Others?

Hurt and pain to victims and those that surround them are a characteristic of premature exposure. A teenager, for example, who gets impregnated at 13 years of age, does not only hurt herself. She endangers her health, destroys her education, embarrasses her parents her family, and disappoints loved ones since she is not adequately prepared to become a mother.

Any step to be taken should be weighed in this light to determine whether it is premature or not. The question to ask yourself is, "Can this exposure affect me negatively or hurt me in any way?" Will it hurt the Body of Christ? Will it hurt my church or my relationship with God? Will it hurt my society, nation or the world? If the answer to any of these questions is yes, then the exposure is premature and the timing at that particular moment is not God-initiated.

Another example is a pastor breaking away or taking a step that causes a church split, leading to the backsliding of many members and creating irreparable damage and hurt. Where the result is this devastating, the timing ought to be seriously considered. The mode of leaving should be carefully examined to make sure that it is in accordance with the will of God.

Ministers, no matter how justifiable the reason might be, God always has perfect timing for your deliverance and relocation. If it is His will, He will perform it, since He is not the author of confusion.

Hagar left Abraham and Sarah because she was treated harshly for despising Sarah. She left prematurely, but the angel of the Lord asked her to go back and submit to Sarah because there still remained a blessing for her in the home of Abraham (Gen. 16:1-14). So, it is all right if one insists that God is asking him to leave. When, where, and how must be very clear, and wisdom must be applied so that it does not hurt innocent people, the ministry, or yourself. You can always close the door behind you without slamming it in anger.

Premature departure has resulted in terrible splits and breakaways that have grieved the Holy Spirit. It has quenched people's anointing, destroyed many before their time, and cruelly divided the Body of Christ.

Jesus said, "My yoke is easy and my burden is light" (Matt. 11:30). Whenever the timing is right, the struggle is not so tedious. It becomes a natural process. This is not to say that the genuine execution of Christian or civil duties is always smooth sailing, characterized by perfect transition. This is not so! Notwithstanding, it is worth mentioning that whenever this should happen to God's people, the Lord gives grace, and brings his assurance again and again. His presence and assurance makes the yoke easier and lightens the weight of the burden, for God does not willingly bring affliction on the sons of men.

Angels ministered to Jesus through hardship, weakness and persecution. The Lord assured Paul that His grace was sufficient for him and on several occasions encouraged him to move on with his work, in spite of the hardships and opposition. The same was true for Peter, Jeremiah, and Ezekiel. Many others received assurances from the Lord, which made the yoke easy and the burden light.

When the hardship seems undue, and the assurances of God are not there, and you are not sure whether it was God who asked you to take those steps, there is a strong probability that what you are going through is a result of premature exposure. Divine assistance must be sought to know how to rectify the situation.

Who Receives the Glory?

Another indicator that can be used is whether the exposure will bring glory to God as opposed to enhancing one's personal fame, image and popularity. If the result is the former, then the timing is right. If it relates more to the latter then the exposure is premature. It could actually be a trap, no matter how legitimate and prospective it looks. This is clearly illustrated in the story about the building of the tower of Babel. They said one to another, "Let us make brick... let us build us a city and a tower whose top may reach unto heaven and let us make us a name lest we be scattered abroad upon the face of the whole earth. (Gen. 11:2-4)"

Here is a clear example where people came together to accomplish something powerful and great. The problem was not the project, but rather the motive, and whom it was to glorify.

David, at the age of 17 took a giant step to risk his life to bring glory to the name of the Lord. David said, "...Who is this uncircumcised Philistine that he should defy the armies of the living God...you come to me with a sword and spear, and with a shield, but I come to thee in the name of the Lord of host" (I Sam. 17:36,45-47).

From the above Scripture we realize that although he was young and appeared inexperienced, the end was real success, which brought joy to all, because it was solely to bring glory to God.

Whenever you are confronted by an exposure that will not glorify God, and serve His purposes, but is self-centered then premature exposure is enticing you. Consent not!

Checking the Roots

In order to apprehend the right timing, one has to check the very root of the exposure. Premature exposure has its roots in three main sources, namely: people, yourself, or the devil.

If the root of an exposure, open door, election, promotion, calling, ordination or opportunity is from the above sources, then the exposure is premature, because it has destructive potential. This is a caution that every child of God, including you my dear friend, should never forget.

Not every promotion, elevation, anointing, blessing or good gift comes from God. The devil can and does release things to meet people's needs as long as it hinders or stops people from giving him a hard time. The devil also gives people gifts. However, his gifts have the potential to distract the recipient from God's path for their life. He does not mind parting with anything as long as he knows it will slow you down or stop you. He said to Jesus, "...whomsoever I will I give it..." which means he has the power to give, but the devil never gives anything for free. He will make sure that whoever receives anything from him pays dearly. God is the best Giver, and every good and perfect gift comes from Him, the Father of lights (James 1:17).

Preachers of the faith, kings and those in authority, politicians, businessmen, family leaders, fathers, mothers and tomorrow's leaders, hear me today! Many are the doors the enemy is opening, to distract you and those who look up to you. Brace yourselves and remember that not every door or opportunity that comes before you is from God. Hold fast, wait, and receive what is of God, "for His blessings maketh rich and addeth no sorrow" (Prov. 10:22). When He opens a door, no one can shut it forever.

Let's look at a few cases from the Bible, mankind's manual, for the roots or sources of opportunities that came the way of people and how they handled it. This will help equip you with practical examples so you know how you can deal with similar situations.

The Devil's Blessing

We have already read one classical example of blessing and exposure that came from the devil. This was in the wilderness when Satan tempted Jesus and tried to offer him the glories and riches of the earth. Jesus knew very well that the gift was from Satan and rejected it. In our time, many people receive gifts from the devil in various forms. It may be money, power, glory, or other things.

Friend, the devil can never out-give God, and Jesus knew this. The fact that the devil was willing to part with that offer meant that if Jesus waited and paid the necessary price, God would offer Him a more powerful and greater glory than what the devil was offering. We see that later, when Jesus, after resurrecting from the dead, declared, "...all power in heaven and earth has been given unto me" (Matt. 28:18).

Self-Origin

There are times when the exposure or move is from self. In his quest for a child, Abraham was convinced by his wife to go in for Hagar, her Egyptian slave, and have a child by her. This resulted in serious physical and spiritual consequences. The physical consequences are the conflicts between the Arab nations and the Jews that still linger until today.

The spiritual consequence was the interference in the fulfillment of God's purposes through the birth order. A critical look at Abraham's descendants reveals some deviation of the birth order because firstborns were supposed to receive the double portion, kingship, and priesthood. However, we see the order being reversed in several instances: Isaac and Ishmael, Jacob and Esau, Judah and Reuben, Ephraim and Manasseh, Moses and Aaron, and David and his brothers.

People's Exposure

Jesus impacted the cities tremendously as he operated in the power of God. On one such occasion, after preaching to over 5000 people, he miraculously fed all the people and had surplus. After this miracle the people wanted to make him king. This was premature exposure and its source was the people. Had he not withdrawn from them, they would have forced Him to be their earthly king. Later we also see Jesus' family pressurizing Him to prematurely expose. Jesus understanding timing said, "My time is not yet..." (John 2:1-11)

If you are destined to be great, beware of people who will try to prematurely expose you into big deals, political appointments and offices, relationships, marriage, ministry, or spiritual office because of what they can get from you. Please be aware that there are many people like that. Always check the root or source of the exposure, whether it's man-centered, self-centered, or the devil's package. Avoid it, because it's a counterfeit. Count on God's blessing and exposure because if the devil or men prematurely expose you, they can also prematurely demote you. You cannot entrust your life and destiny in the hands of men! It is always better to fall into the hands of God because He is merciful and his gifts and callings are without repentance.

Chapter 8

Solutions to Premature Exposure

To every question there is an answer and to every problem a solution. Let us attempt to propound some divine solutions to this whole subject of premature exposure. God's word, which is a lamp unto our feet, and a light unto your path, is our main source. In the same way that He sent His Word, the Word of the Lord comes to you. It will heal you and deliver you from the destruction that premature exposure has made you liable to.

Let see a typical case from the scriptures:

And he said, "A certain man has two sons; and the younger of them said to his father, "Father, give me the portion of goods that falleth to me". And he divided them his living. Not many days after, the younger son gathered all he had together and took his journey in to a far country and there wasted his substance with riotous living. And when he had spent all there arose a mighty famine in that land and he began to be in want. And he went and joined himself to a citizen of that country; and he sent him into his fields to feed swine. And he would fain have filled his belly with the husks that the swine did eat; and no man gave unto him. (Luke 15:11-16)

This gives us a dramatic picture of premature exposure. It shows its consequences and, thankfully, the way out. It presented to us this young man obsessed with a strong desire, which eventually led to his premature exposure. The son left the family with an inheritance, which, I believe, the father reluctantly released to him.

People who prematurely expose themselves are usually compelled by selfish motives. Like this young man those who prematurely expose themselves think what they are doing is right. It becomes very difficult to convince them otherwise, as any such attempt is interpreted as jealousy or a lack of understanding. Not long afterwards the son began to face the consequences of his action. He squandered all his wealth and began to suffer.

"When he came to his senses, he said I will set out and go back to my father and say to him father, I have sinned against Heaven and against you". He immediately came to his senses as a result of his distress. If for any reason, you are suffering as a result of premature exposure, let this chapter come to you as help. Let us systematically follow the steps he took when he came to his senses.

He reflected over the situation and then made a decision. A wrong way will definitely lead you to the wrong place. If you want to go to the right place, you must quit the wrong way and start on the right way. This comes by stopping to reflect and to take closer look. When you are on a highway and realize that you are driving in the opposite direction of where you should actually be going, what do you do? The natural thing is to stop, probably investigate to ascertain where you went wrong and seek confirmation pertaining to the right direction. You then turn around completely and start heading towards the right direction.

Premature exposure can be likened to moving in a direction that takes one out of God's pathway; like the younger prodigal son, after acknowledging your state, stop, reflect and ask yourself some questions. Stop to analyze your pace, stop to ascertain whether you have really gone the way God wants you to. Every now and then we need to stop. When you are on the right path you do not need to stop. However, when you are on the wrong path, it is wise to stop.

Please make it a habit to pause for reflection every now and then, to make sure that every thing is on course; it may be concerning your life, family, marriage, health, business, ministry, career, and relationship with God, political pursuit or even in your body. Some may not see the wisdom in this, but it is very crucial when it comes to premature exposure.

You must then discover where you went wrong. If you do not know where you went wrong you cannot intelligently rectify the situation. It is also crucial and strategic to the next step in the process of establishing your change. Take time to find out and write it down so that you can deal with the issue, leaving no grounds uncovered. After that the prodigal son made a decision. The battle should be won in the mind before it can be won outside. Therefore, make a decision and be prepared to take responsibility for your decisions; and do not change in the face of pressure or adversity. Your decisions are very important especially those based on God's word and principles.

The prodigal son made a decision to confess his sin and repent. Confession and repentance are key decisions one has to make. True repentance signifies turning around completely and forsaking the old way. One has to acknowledge that premature exposure is sin. It is because such exposure usually originates from the devil and the flesh, motivated by greed, covetousness, jealousy and the desire for instant pleasure. This is sin and its wages is death. Therefore, if you have acknowledged your sins and where you went wrong, humbly repent before God. The young man did exactly that when he said, "I will arise and go to my father, I will say unto him father I have sinned against heaven and before thee".

I say to you, the Lord has no "pleasure in the death of the wicked (sinner) but that the wicked turns from his ways and live. Turn yea from your evil ways for why will ye die" (Ezekiel 33:11). God has no pleasure in the death of your ministry, political career, marriage or anything the concerns you. Repent and life will follow.

True repentance leads to refreshment. For he said "...and I will say unto him father I have sinned against heaven and before thee". I believe that his acknowledgment that he had not only sinned against his father but also against Heaven made him repent to God first and later to his father. After making the decision he humbled himself and said, "...am no more worthy to be called thy son make me one of thy hired servants" [vrs.18-19].

You need humility before you can repent before God and man. Humility is the key to being exalted by God, no matter how you might have fallen. Pride will keep you far away from God. Humility will release you into His grace and mercy, which every one needs in order to "make it", for God gives grace to the humble but resists the proud. God cannot humble you. Nobody can humble anybody. The best thing any one can do is to humiliate you or disgrace you. You have to humble yourself. Be ready to humble yourself before God and those you have offended through your action. For he said, "I have sinned, make me as one of your hired servants."

After deciding to repent take action, because the decision alone is not enough. After you repent, deal with the consequences of your action in prayer or take physical steps. The Word of God talks about "the curse of the law" which moves into operation as a result of one's previous action. This is the principle of sowing and reaping that can be turned for good through prayer and appropriating the blood of the lamb.

One has to sometimes take physical and practical measures to deal with the consequences. Zaccheus for example had to pay back all the money he had stolen after encountering Jesus and he was blessed. You also need to take physical steps to rectify the situation and to pacify the grieved. Through prayer and appropriating the blood of Jesus, one is justified.

Christ through the shedding of His blood has redeemed us from the curse of the law. For He became a curse for us that we may inherit the blessings of Abraham for "cursed is anyone that hangs on a tree" [Col 3:15]. That was the price Jesus paid for you. By hanging on the cross, He released you from every curse. The prodigal son took a step to put his decisions to work, he journeyed back and acknowledged to God and his father that he had sinned. He humbled himself.

After that one needs to inquire of the Lord for the right direction pertaining to what to do and which way to turn. This is because God has the original plan and blue print for your life. When you receive the answer do not shelve it, no matter how small it might seem to you. Revelation is progressive. God reveals a little to you to see what you will do with it. So obey what He is telling you and physically take steps to put it into practice and move. You will come to realize that things are getting better.

This is the general way employed in dealing with premature exposure. The results are outstanding and unbelievable. This is the portion of everyone that applies the principle that the young man applied. Jesus recommended this as an example for all, including you.

The scripture records that "when he was a great way off his father saw him and had compassion". This, to me, says it is God's will to see you out of your mess. It is His desire to see you changed and blessed. God's mercy is for those who have gone far off. He knows your state and sees you coming back. This should encourage your heart.

It continues to say that his father had compassion, which means that his bowels were already filled with mercy, grace, and love, which made him identify or feel the pain the his son went through. God, our Heavenly Father, identifies with the pain you have been through and feels compassion towards you.

No matter what your fault and sin may be, He is full of compassion and he waits to express it to you. Compassion awaits you, not judgment and rejection. Don't ever think that God will reject or accuse you when you apply the principles above. He will not reject those who come to him.

Many may desire to see you punished but God, in his mercy will not do this. He would rather have compassion. I can hear someone saying, "Bishop you do not understand that my case is so serious. I have not even told anybody about it. I don't think God will forgive me." My dear friend, God can and has already paid the price for that sin also. His forgiveness and grace are greater than all of your sins.

The young man's father ran "and fell on the shoulders of his son and kissed him." God's compassion is being exposed through this book he is bringing you to himself right now. You may be coming, unsure, and wondering, with a lot of questions on your mind. But listen friend; God is not only standing, waiting for you to come; He is running to you! You may be slow in your pace but God is running to you because He loves you and wants to see you out of that difficult condition.

God is willing to fall on your neck, and identify with you. His arms are stretched out ready to embrace you. And that is not all. The father gave charge to his servants to take care of him. Angels have been given charge concerning you. The host of heaven is constantly around you to ensure that the Father's will is done.

"Bring forth the best cloth and put it on him". That was one of the things the father asked the servants to do for the prodigal son. God will ask that they robe you. Robe represents your covering, your glory, your dignity, image, and identity.

Premature marital, financial, spiritual and political exposure may have resulted in you, loosing your glory, image, honor, and identity. Restoration awaits you. All you need to do is yield to God's principles. Stretch forth your hands to heaven and give him thanks for this second surprise, oh glory!

"Put a ring on his hand". You may have lost your authority as a spiritual leader, as a husband, wife, or any leadership position that you may have had. But get ready. God will restore your authority and placement, for He said, "behold I give you authority". If it is He that gives, then He will give you back your authority.

Shoes will be put on your feet, which represent a change in your walk and your ways for the better, to walk like the son of a great king. Your walk will be restored, and you will walk in righteousness, holiness, obedience, purity and walk upon your high places. You will walk in corridors of power and walk worthy of His name. God will establish your feet and direct your path.

"And he said bring hither the fatted calf," a representation of the restoration of daily provision or bread. Your hunger will be satisfied and every necessity of life will be restored to you. Divine provision will be your portion. The restoration process will not stop there but will continue to flow because God is a more-than-enough God.

"And let us celebrate and feast". This represents the restoration of his joy and that of others. Those who were afflicted by your premature exposure will now have joy. Their laughter and yours shall be restored. You were lost but you would have been found; you may have been dead, but now you would be alive; your political career, your business, marital life, ministry and everything may have decayed and rotted away but now, it would be alive forever. In Jesus name receive grace and be empowered supernaturally to follow the above principles and continue in them.

God bless you my friend. Please don't stop after reading this book. Use it as a prayer manual and enforce your portion on your knees till you see a manifestation. Remember only the violent take it by force. This may be your portion but you are to take it by force. May your life never be the same again!